STORIES MY FRIENDS LOVE TO HEAR

Joellen Bard

All rights reserved, including the right to reproduce any section of this book, including photography, on any platform.

Copyright © 2018 by Joellen Bard

Cover and Book Design	Joellen Bard
Electronic Formatting	David Bard
Cover Photograph	Adela Serna

Photo on page 59 reproduced with permission from Southern Plains Photography

Photo on page 71 reproduced with permission from the *New York Daily News*

Photo on page 169 reproduced with permission from Barbra Streisand

Photo on page 229 reproduced with permission from Canine Associates

ISBN: 978-0692124765
ISBN: 0692124764

Library of Congress Control Number: 2018906594

Books may be ordered from Amazon.com

Printed in the United States of America

This book is dedicated to my late husband, Arthur Bard, who loved to write and always inspired me to write.

INTRODUCTION

Storytelling is defined as the act of describing an incident or event that has taken place–an event that has the potential to interest, to amuse or to impart a message to another human being.

Joellen Bard is an artist, retired art teacher, author, mother and grandmother, with a wealth of stories to share. She has organized them into anecdotes about life in general, human and animal behavior, school experiences, people she has met, and stories that have been told to her by others. Some stories are funny, some ironic and many show surprising elements of coincidence or unexpected and unexplainable timing in nature.

The importance of storytelling in our daily lives is often underestimated. The psychological benefits of both telling and hearing stories retold have been recognized since ancient times. Such stories transcend many generations and help bind families and cultures; they help us to communicate and understand other people's perspectives.

Different parts of the brain are stimulated when hearing a story. While the language-processing parts in our brains are working, other areas in our brains that are involved in the experience being described are also stimulated. The unconscious mind is always operating, even when we don't know it.

Eyewitness reports often differ and can't fully be relied upon in a forensic setting. That is because the "realities" that each person brings to a situation makes it seem slightly different from another person's recollection of the same experience.

Despite variations in detail, the act of retelling a story serves a vital purpose in our lives. At times like the present when the world seems to be characterized by chaos and random patterns of human behavior, storytelling helps us to have hope for the future and a greater feeling of control over our lives.

Susan Blank, MD (psychiatrist)

AUTHOR'S NOTES

This book is not an autobiography, but it is autobiographical. I cannot tell jokes, but my friends tell me that I tell good stories–that I often make them laugh and think.

This project has been brewing for over 20 years, first as funny stories emanating from teaching experiences, then expanding to include my life experiences and those of others. It has forced me to research the background of the stories about people I have known and things I have done. All these stories are true!

I have so many stories to tell; some people have so few. Seeing through the eyes of an artist, perhaps I learned from my father, "We have to focus mind and eye to uncover and savor the spices of life."

I've decided to share these funny, ironic and sometimes awe-inspiring stories. Each has been audience tested. Unless there was a strong reaction such as wow, oh my, oh my God, or a laugh, I have not included the story.

I thank the many people who have told me their stories and the many people who have listened to my recitations. Except for the section "Name Dropping," all stories are anonymous and nameless. I apologize if someone is offended by names, ethnic references or similarity of story.

I want to thank Dr. Susan Blank for reading the manuscript as it evolved and for providing the Introduction, Nancy Goodman and Millicent McKinley for providing photographs and for reading the manuscript several times, Dorothy Krugman for providing moral support, and Howard Cohen for proofreading. A thank you also goes to my son, David Bard, and my granddaughter, Hannah Bard, for technical support. And a special thank you to my editor, Eliza Shallcross, whose writing knowledge has been invaluable and whose patience has been unending. (Please note: I assume responsibility for any errors.)

I hope that my stories help to conjure up your stories. Stories connect the generations, and I hope that you share "things that you might have forgotten" with family and friends. In the busy age of Facebook, Twitter, reality TV, and real-time coverage of events, we find little time for introspection. Play the remembering game. It has made me happy and kept me stable in times of stress. I hope it can do the same for you.

CONTENTS

LIFE STORIES

    General   3

    Art   31

    Natural Phenomena   45

    Tragedies   61

    Transportation   79

    Travel   101

ANIMAL STORIES   113

SCHOOL STORIES   143

NAME DROPPING   167

STORIES I'VE HEARD   185

LIFE
STORIES

THE PICK-UP

My uncle was in a hospital on the east side of Manhattan. I don't remember which one or why he was there, but I cannot forget this story:

My uncle called from the hospital and told me that my aunt, who was quite heavy, had fallen out of her bed at home. She must have been holding the phone since she was able to call him. My uncle had asked the hospital to discharge him so he could go home and lift his wife off the floor, but they had refused. He thought I should come to discharge him and take him home to help his wife.

I said, "No, I'll come to the hospital to fetch the key to your apartment and I'll go pick her up." I lived near the hospital and they didn't live far away, just across the 59th Street Bridge in Queens. He wouldn't let me do that, so I angrily hung up.

My uncle got dressed, left the hospital without permission, and took a cab to Queens. He told the cab to wait, picked his wife up, took the cab back to the hospital, got undressed and got back into bed.

The hospital never missed him!

A TREE GROWS IN...

My mother always grew avocado plants in our Brooklyn apartment. She placed an avocado pit on three large toothpicks in a glass. I told her that it looked like a "pot" plant, not that I knew what a marijuana plant looked like at that time.

I used the same planting method in our winter Florida apartment until one day when my Jamaican friend walked in. She said, "Let me take it to my garden. Girl, it needs soil and sun." She owns a beautiful house with a large Caribbean garden in a gated community in Miramar where she grows bananas, pineapple, soursop and white sweet potatoes as well as avocados.

Three years later, a package arrived in New York City–two Haas avocados from "my tree." It was now more than 15 feet tall and lived next to her Florida avocado tree. Neighbors came to her backyard and took avocados as they fell from the tree. The avocados from these two trees fed the neighborhood.

This tree bore so much fruit and grew so tall over the past few years that people couldn't reach to pick the avocados, even on a ladder. My friend's husband wanted to cut it down, but my friend said, "You cannot cut down Joellen's tree."

The final chapter of my avocado tree: Hurricane Irma, in September 2017, destroyed everything in my friend's yard. My tree lost all of its leaves and branches and leaned precariously towards her house. My friend's husband got his wish fulfilled–my tree needed to be chopped down. And it was!

The final, final chapter: my friend called me to ask, "How do you start an avocado plant?"

Update July 9, 2018: in the spot where the tree was chopped down, a new avocado tree has grown. My new avocado tree is already eight feet and bearing fruit. Amazing!

GARBAGE TICKET

I don't know of anyone who ever received a garbage ticket, but me.

The president of the neighborhood association in my community in Brooklyn decided that the homeowners didn't remove their garbage cans from curbside fast enough. He told the sanitation department to issue tickets when cans were left past a certain hour.

One day, I didn't remove my can and received a $60 ticket. (By the way, this was when everyone used metal cans.) Why didn't I remove the can? I didn't know that the garbage had been collected because the cover was on the can. Usually the cover was strewn in the gutter and was often run over by the sanitation truck.

I went to court with Exhibit A, a flattened garbage can cover. When I showed my exhibit, there was hysteria in the courtroom. I don't think the judge had ever seen evidence like that. As everyone roared with laughter, the judge proclaimed, "case dismissed."

The representative from the sanitation department was not happy with this decision. The president of the association, who was a neighbor, couldn't believe that I was the one who got a ticket. The sanitation department was told not to issue any more tickets.

Photography by Joellen Bard

THE CACTUS FLOWER

I awoke one morning. There it was—one beautiful big white flower on my cylindrical cactus plant. I immediately fetched my camera and took a picture.

When I returned home from work that evening, the flower had already died. This cactus flowered one time for one day in ten years, and it did not survive my move from Manhattan to New Jersey in 2006. But it is immortalized in my painting *Still Life with Cactus*. A photograph of the flower will have to suffice here; the painting does not reproduce well in black and white.

GRANDCHILDREN STORIES

SHRINKING

"Grandma, lie down on the floor, I want to measure you," said my four-year-old granddaughter. She measured me with her roll-out tape measure and announced, "You are a little over 60 inches."

"I used to be five feet two inches," I said, "but now I am five feet one inch or less."

"Grandma, you shouldn't take so many showers."

TAKE HIM BACK

We babysat our granddaughter, age two, while our daughter-in-law gave birth to a second child, a boy. Home they came from the hospital, proud mother and father and baby brother. Our granddaughter, who had seen her brother at the hospital the day before, took one look at the new arrival and calmly made what sounded like a prepared statement, "Take him back where he came from."

Later that year, she proclaimed, "Put him in an envelope and give it to the mailman."

Teenagers now, they are the best of friends.

EARLY READER

At age four, our granddaughter was very excited. She read her first sentence:

4U2P

These letters were written above each stall in a lady's room on the island of Jamaica. I guess that was a kind of international language.

THE ROBBER

My grandson, age five, was watching a video called *The Three Robbers*. He was so impressed with this Robin Hood-like story that when it ended he pronounced, "When I grow up, I think I want to be a robber."

MT. OLYMPUS

I lived in a dorm on Mt. Olympus my freshman year at Syracuse University. There were 500 covered steps to climb to reach the beautiful new freshman dormitory.

Wanting to know the thoughts of freshmen, many away from home for the first time, the guidance department placed a "Dream Box" on a table in the front lobby. It became the fad–every morning all the freshmen girls on my floor fed the box with their dreams. I didn't have any dreams to report. Until this day, I rarely remember my dreams. So instead, I invented dreams.

I do not remember the dreams I concocted, but they were so creative that I should have handed them in to my freshman English teacher. I did poorly writing responses to questions like, "Why or why not would you like to be an earthworm?" My made-up dreams, I think, would have received A's.

ODDS

What are the odds that three of nine children in the same family would have the same birthday? My husband has one niece and eight nephews. Two of the nephews and our son, three cousins, were born on the same day each six years apart–1957, 1963, 1969, our son being the youngest of this trio. I find that those odds are too difficult to calculate!

At Syracuse University, I had a dorm-mate and friend who was born on the same day, in the same year, at the same hospital in Brooklyn. We always kidded that we had been switched at birth. Amazingly, our names were also very similar. Our last names were spelled differently, but they were both pronounced "Ubin." We laughed a lot about this coincidence. But, I always thought, maybe, we really were switched at birth, until my son was an adult. He looks so much like my father that he could stand in a picture with my father and his two brothers and pass for the fourth brother. I guess I wasn't switched at birth.

RETAIL MATH

We've all run into this: the computer caused the problem. This becomes a great excuse for the uncaring, incompetent or inexperienced worker.

Recently, I bought a pair of pants in a major department store using that department store's credit card. I rarely return purchased merchandise, but this time I decided that the pants did not fit properly and I returned them.

The original price of the item was $69.99, but on a special sale they were $39.99. I had used a $5.00 store coupon as well, so I paid $34.99, a real bargain.

I tried to return the pants. First, I was told that the item number was incorrect, so they could not refund my money. Whose fault was that, certainly not mine? I had the right receipt, because I had never removed it from the bag. Then, I tried to exchange the pants for another size. The computer wouldn't let them do that either.

"Can't you override the computer?" I asked. "No," said the department manager.

After much hassle, they finally let me return the pants.

I paid $34.99 and I received a credit for $39.99. They did not make a mistake. That was the only way the computer could do this transaction. I received $5.00 too much and the store lost a sale.

This story does not end here. I received the statement for my store card in the mail. They credited me $55.00, the whole amount I had spent that day, not $39.99.

And, along with online sales, we wonder why so many stores are going out of business.

NO SALE

I've designed, made, and sold adult and children's knitwear privately and in boutiques for a very long time. In fact, I studied knitwear design at FIT (Fashion Institute of Technology) when on a teaching sabbatical.

People often ask where I get my yarn. The answer is locally and all over the world, transported by friends or when I travel. How excited I am when a package arrives from "God knows where." Once, my friend sent a package of beautiful merino wool from New Zealand, and I loved it so much that I wanted more. Since the yarn store's telephone number was on the receipt, I called the store in New Zealand to place a large order. They told me they couldn't sell it to me.

"What," I heard myself screaming. "Why?"

They responded that I had to buy it in the Western Hemisphere and they directed me to a company in Canada. This company did not have nor could they order that yarn.

I don't know what global trade deal that was or if it still exists, but I question whether it was good for America or for that matter for the global economy. It certainly was not good for me!

MYSTERY

Every family has secrets and mysteries–there is a mystery in my father's family history. I will never know the answer.

I have conflicting information about where my father's family lived in East New York, Brooklyn. First, I heard that they moved from apartment to apartment every time an apartment needed painting. Then I heard that they originally owned a four-family house which they sold and replaced with a one-family house. This is supposedly how they survived the Depression.

I will also never know where the fruit store, shown below, was located. My grandfather, who is in this picture, owned four different fruit and vegetable stores in East New York at different times.

This photograph hangs in my apartment. Every time I pass this photograph, I say, "Where was that?"

Photograph from the family archive

OLD TIMES/NEW TIMES

In the early 1960s, I worked for John Wiley and Sons, a large book publishing company, during each summer of my college years. For the first two years, we did the billing by hand. Then came the new computing machinery for billing. The computer, using punch cards, filled a large room. We were all awed by so much equipment to produce a single bill. We also thought about our jobs being replaced by machines. I think of the small size of computers now–how fast technology has accelerated since the 1960s.

I recently looked on the internet to see the difference in prices of food and household objects in the 1940s and 1950s, when I was a child, as compared to prices today. I was amazed. It's worth a look if this information interests you.

However, I will share my own experiences. I remember a Good Humor ice cream pop was 5 cents, lunch of a tuna fish sandwich and a Coke in a local sandwich shop was 35 cents, and a Spaulding ball was 5 cents.

My father bought our first television set when I was eight years old. It was a ten-inch Dumont with a magnifying glass covering the screen. Our TV antenna was the first on the roof of our apartment house. Soon after, the number of "rabbit ears" on the roof began to grow. (My brother-in-law had the first color television in the family many years later. We weren't allowed to sit too close or, it was believed, we might get cancer.)

I remember ice being delivered and the iceman cutting ice on his truck in Brooklyn. We had a refrigerator in the 1940s, but many didn't. In fact, my aunt's rented summer home in Pennsylvania had an icebox, a large wooden cabinet with many doors. Those cabinets today are treasured antiques used for storage or media centers in living rooms.

I remember coal pouring down the chute of our apartment house. I remember the fish man, the vegetable man, and the knife-sharpening man doing business from a truck. I remember diapers being delivered and diaper companies claiming that paper diapers would do harm to babies.

I remember that Syracuse University in 1959 was $3500 for tuition, room and board. It is now $62,000. That's hard to believe, but true. The starting salary for my first teaching job in 1964 was $5,000 per year. The starting salary for teachers in the New York City school system is now $54,000. And our first new car, bought in 1963, was $3500. My new car in 2017 was $30,000.

Times have certainly changed. I conclude: life is very different in the 21st century.

FURNITURE

When we bought our Brooklyn house, we bought an English dining room table and the fixture hanging above from the previous owner. We had no chairs or breakfront. The chairs we bought in an antique store on Broadway, but the breakfront was another matter. Any antique ranged from $10,000 to $14,000.

One afternoon, my husband called and said, "I bought a second-hand breakfront on Broadway for $75. I'm coming home on a truck with it." The truck arrived with my husband sitting on the breakfront which was this beautiful dark oak piece of furniture. It was perfect and it did go in the dining room. My husband thought if we didn't put it in the dining room, we'd use it as a bookcase in the basement. It was a real antique from the early 1900s–a breakfront that they had used as a candy counter in Schrafft's restaurant on lower Broadway which was going out of business. There were holes in some of the shelves to help candy boxes stand.

When we moved from Manhattan to New Jersey in 2006, we had no place for the breakfront. We approached Sotheby's auction house knowing that we owned a piece of Americana. We didn't have documentation of provenance, so the breakfront was worthless. We donated it.

When we moved, we also sold many other antiques to an antique dealer. We sold two 1930s Italian wrought-iron chairs with brass arms and horse-head finials. Six months later, I just happened to pick up a copy of *Architectural Digest*. There were my chairs in the magazine. What a coincidence!

COINICIDENCE

I found a watch that I hadn't worn in years. I said to myself, "Gee, this is nice; I should wear it." I marveled that the time was correct, 8:00 am. "I guess the battery is still working." I put the watch on. When I checked with the wall clock a half hour later, the watch still showed 8:00. I guess the battery wasn't working. What a coincidence that the watch had stopped at 8:00, the exact time I had looked at it

A week later, Daylight Savings Time began. I tried to change the time on my watch, but the stem would not turn. Therefore, I found another old watch to use until I had my good watch fixed. This watch said 10:00, but all my clocks said 9:00. I assumed that the battery wasn't working. It was. It was 10:00 am Daylight Savings Time. I had forgotten to change the clocks.

Two similar coincidences involving time happened in one week. Amazing!

PAPER DOLLS

My mother bought me a present. It was something she thought was very novel–a paper dress. This cellulose technology was patented in 1958. I was in high school at the time, and I don't remember where she bought it. I thought of this story recently when looking through the spring fashion magazines. The vibrant print fabrics now being shown reminded me of that flowery yellow two-piece dress. You could wash it a couple of times and then you were supposed to throw it away and replace it. I remember that it was cheap, so "throw away and replace garments" had potential. But it was never successfully marketed and was gone from the fashion scene by 1967. (For more information about the history of paper clothing, look under paper clothing on the internet.)

I washed the dress a couple of times and then as predicted, it needed to be thrown out. I liked it and thought the concept was unique. I wanted to replace it, but the item was no longer available.

YOU CAN'T MAKE THAT UP

I put on an old rain jacket that I bought in Vancouver a long time ago, along with a big floppy matching hat. The fabric of this jacket is shiny chintz with a very busy blue, aqua, lavender and yellow floral pattern. I hadn't worn it for years, but those patterns are now back in vogue.

I had a doctor's appointment and the nurse commented on the jacket. I told her this story:

My niece threw a big birthday party for her daughter in their backyard in Long Island. There were at least 20 tables with balloons flying and, believe it or not, tablecloths made of the exact same fabric as my jacket. I couldn't believe it! I visited my niece with the jacket before she returned the rented party stuff, and we had another good laugh.

The nurse said, "You can't make things like that up."

LUCK

In catastrophic times, wars, hurricanes, earthquakes, etc., luck determines whether you live or die! Even in normal times, luck plays a big role in our lives.

A NEAR-DEATH EXPERIENCE

I was driving on the Brooklyn-Queens Expressway, which is a raised highway, heading for the Brooklyn Battery Tunnel to Manhattan. An exit was closed and traffic pylons had been placed at the exit. I was in the left lane against the side railing of the highway. An 18-wheeler–either because it had hit a pylon or was trying to avoid a pylon–jack-knifed into my lane and stopped. I didn't hit him and thank goodness he didn't hit me. If this had happened one split second later, I would have been crushed against the side railing of that highway or even have fallen completely off the road.

    Luck was with me that day!

OUR LAST FLORIDA TRIP

In 2015, our flight to Florida was canceled due to snow. The airline called us just as we were ready to leave the house and said, "The flight is canceled; do not come to the airport unless you have a confirmed flight." After much ado, we were finally re-ticketed for a flight five days later.

Before our original flight, here was my to-do list–put keys away, turn off water, turn thermostat down, take checkbook, put telephone, television and internet on vacation, have mail forwarded, take glasses, take medicine, give extra food to friends and family.

After the flight was canceled, here was my new to-do list– take out keys, turn on water, turn thermostat up, put checkbook back in desk drawer, put medicine back in kitchen closet, turn telephone, television and internet on, buy food, forget about mail.

Five days later and ready to leave again. Here was my to-do list–put keys away, turn off water, turn thermostat down, take medicine, take glasses, take checkbook, put telephone, television and internet back on vacation, throw food out!

Perhaps, it would have been easier to go to the airport and stay there.

Circumstances kept us from leaving earlier in December, so that was our last winter in Florida. We were not lucky that time. We sold our Florida condo.

NO CHECK

We ate a good meal with friends in an Upper West Side restaurant in Manhattan.

After we had finished eating, we waited and waited but no check came. A waiter finally told us that the computer had broken. The owner wasn't there, nor could they contact him. They couldn't write out all of the checks by hand. They didn't know what to do, so they did nothing.

After at least an hour, we figured our approximate bill, put our money on the table and left.

I wonder what other customers did, and I wonder how many people ate for free that night.

MONEY LAUNDERING

Not once but twice, my husband took his wallet for a swim in our condominium's pool in Florida because he had forgotten to take it out of his bathing suit pocket. As we put the bills out to dry, we laughed. He did a good job of laundering money.

SPILLED WINE

We were with friends out West. I don't remember whether we were in a restaurant in Bryce or Zion National Park, but I do remember the beautiful canyon view with eagles flying by.

My husband spilled red wine. This time, luckily, not on me. Then my friend's husband spilled his glass of red wine too. What a mess! The waiter just looked and looked, and finally said, "I guess we'd better give you a new table."

I don't think we were liked very much in that restaurant, but when we arrived at our new table, the waiter brought us two glasses of wine. This time it was white.

AB

My husband, Arthur Bard, always told me that he had blood type AB Positive which is rare. One day, I looked at his medical record and realized that he actually had blood type O which is common. The AB on his record were his initials, not his blood type.

THE STAR-SPANGLED BANANA

My first name and those of my father and mother created the perfect acronym for my family's singing group: J. A. and M. for Joellen, Alma and Milton. We'd have J.A.M. sessions often, and laughed at our horrible voices. We'd choose difficult songs to sing on purpose like "The Star- Spangled Banner," so we could laugh harder. We even tried to determine who had the worst voice. We never succeeded–all our voices were bad. But we had lots of fun.

When my father developed kidney stones, he always blamed me, although the doctor repeatedly told him the stones were composed of chocolate and nuts. But my dad honestly believed that running after me while teaching me to ride a two-wheeler at age seven caused his kidney stones.

What I will never forget, though, was that when he was so sick and maybe delirious, he lay in bed singing, with his lousy voice, "The Star-Spangled Banana."

Art

FAMOUS ARTISTS

My studio was in our converted garage with a skylight and heat. At one point, I needed more space for the ten-foot paintings I was producing. I didn't want to rent space in Soho where I exhibited because I wanted to work near home. I wanted to paint when I got the urge to do so.

We searched for a larger house but never found one. We did, however, have interesting experiences: the house with clothing stacked from ceiling to floor in every room and the funeral director's house with three black bathrooms. And the best was the one with the artwork.

We walked into a non-assuming house with the real estate agent. Above the mantle was a large Modigliani nude woman which I thought was a reproduction. My husband, the real estate agent and the owner proceeded upstairs; I remained downstairs in awe of my finds. There was a beautiful small Braque cubist oil painting in the dining room, and an extremely large Picasso drawing in the living room. And there were many more paintings and drawings by known artists. I touched the Braque, something I always wanted to do in a museum. Authentication is not my thing, and even museums make mistakes, but these seemed to be originals.

I screamed, "They're real," at the top of my lungs.

I think I scared everyone upstairs. The owner came running down.

"Yes, they are real," he said. "Most people don't know."

The Modigliani was as fine as any I've seen in books or in museums around the world. "What are they doing here?" I asked.

"My parents bought them in Paris in 1905 for very little." This collection is priceless! I ponder, "Where is this priceless collection now? Has it been exhibited?"

But, I still can't believe that these important and beautiful works of art were in a house in Brooklyn.

All I can say about that experience is WOW!

EMBASSIES

DENMARK

I was exhibiting my artwork in a gallery in Brooklyn Heights in the 1970s when a couple purchased a mixed-media sculpture from my *River Series*. This free-hanging wall sculpture consisted of three plexiglass tubes with painted and sewn canvas swirled within. They told me that they owned an apartment in Copenhagen that had a round room in a turret, and that this artwork was perfect for that space.

Twenty-five years later, I received a phone call from the same couple. They would be in New York for a few years–he had become the cultural attaché for the Danish government. They were living in the Danish residence on the Upper East Side of Manhattan, and they invited my husband and me to come have a drink with them.

We walked into that beautiful house where they were living, and there on the large staircase hung my three tubes. They told me they had lived in many countries during the past 25 years, and had always specially packed my artwork and taken it with them on airplanes so it wouldn't be damaged.

UNITED STATES

In 1976, I took an ad in *Cue Magazine*: if someone could offer me something other than money for my artwork, I would consider the offer.

Soon after, I received a phone call from the State Department in Washington. The U.S. cultural attaché came to New York to see me about a project.

The result of that meeting was a large piece entitled *Especially for Tehran*, sewn fabric stretching from ceiling to floor. It hung in the U.S. Embassy in Tehran.

In 1978, I received a package in the mail–my artwork with an explanation about its return. "We are afraid to keep it–we know that the Shah is in trouble and we don't know what is going to happen." We, of course, now know that there was a revolution in Iran in 1979. The Shah, who was supported by the United States, was replaced with an Islamist, Ayatollah Khomeini, and an Islamist Republic.

The piece always held special significance for me. I exhibited *Especially for Tehran* only once since then. Included in the exhibit was all the correspondence from the State Department. After the exhibit, I neatly folded the sewn canvas, and put the piece back in the box in which it had been returned. It has been there ever since!

NAKED / NUDE

At the Art Students League, in the live drawing class that I attended, the models would pose nude. They remained nude during breaks, but they made sure all the window shades were down.

◎

At Syracuse University Art School, the first day of nude drawing class, the 18-year-old boys were goo-goo-eyed when they saw a nude female model. I still laugh when I think of them, but I also laugh at myself because I behaved not much better years later.

In New York State at that time, male nude figures were required to wear jockstraps. Females were totally nude. Why this was so, I will never know.

After two master's degrees and many years later, I was enrolled in a scholarship painting program at the Brooklyn Museum. A nude male model appeared, without a jockstrap. Not only was I shocked because he was totally nude, but I'd never seen an uncircumcised penis except in marble. I guess the jockstrap law had changed.

I was as goo-goo-eyed as those 18-year-old boys.

◎

My husband and I stayed at an upscale hotel in Rome with a beautiful swimming facility. I had finished swimming and decided to shower in the locker room. There were two clearly marked locker rooms, male and female, on either side of the pool. I proceeded to the female room and took my shower in a large uncurtained stall. I walked out nude just as a nude man walked out of the adjacent stall.

I guess the Europeans didn't care which locker room they used. For an American in 1985, this was a shocker!

When I returned from studying in France in the early 1960s, my parents and I spent a weekend in Asbury Park, New Jersey. I had bought a bikini in France. It was really a two-piece suit which wasn't very revealing–it was a cute light brown suit with white lace and the bottom came up to the waist. I wore it to the beach and was told that bikinis were not allowed. I thought the lifeguard was kidding me, so I tried another beach. They didn't let me stay there either.

It's hard to believe that that bathing suit was unacceptable. Times have really changed.

Photography by Arthur Bard

ART EXHIBIT

At one of my first solo art exhibits in an art gallery in New York City's Soho, my father "pulled a fast one."

I was surprised that I sold as well as I did at that exhibit. There were paintings, but primarily prints that weren't too expensive.

Years later, my father told me what he had done: he walked on Wooster Street where the gallery was located and gave money to strangers to buy my artwork. These people, he told me, thought he was crazy, but they did come and buy. I know from where his idea came. I heard this story many times, but never put two and two together. His friend's daughter was an actress. For one of her performances, her father was responsible for packing the theater.

My father's act was a magnanimous gesture. It would have been nicer if he had kept his mouth shut and not told me what he had done.

ETHICS

SYRACUSE UNIVERSITY

When I was studying art at Syracuse University, a doctoral candidate had painted a 10' x 14' painting of the art faculty, full body portraits standing in a group. This was the equivalent of a doctoral thesis. I remember that it was a beautiful painting.

The administration wanted to hang that monumental painting permanently in the lobby of the art building. "Not without payment," said the artist. The school would not pay for her painting, so she cut it into tiny pieces in front of their eyes and mine.

Whether she received her doctorate in fine arts degree, I do not remember.

PRATT INSTITUTE

When I was studying painting at Pratt Institute, I had a solo painting and drawing exhibit in one of Pratt's galleries. When the exhibit ended, the paintings and drawings were returned to me, but two were missing. I asked where the two paintings were, but I never got an answer.

One day, a closet in the hallway was open. There, standing on the floor near the door, were my two missing paintings. I was so angry that no one had asked me if they could keep the paintings that I stole them from the closet. I'm sure they never missed the paintings I retrieved.

In retrospect, I wonder why they wanted those paintings. Could someone have wanted to promulgate them, or did someone think I'd become famous and they'd become rich? I know for a fact that art schools are constantly in need of storage space. In the end, they probably would have been thrown out.

PRICELESS

The dictionary defines "priceless" as: "having a value beyond any price; invaluable." I learned in art school that Leonardo da Vinci's *Mona Lisa*, the most famous painting in the world, was priceless.

On November 15, 2017, da Vinci's portrait of Jesus, *Salvator Mundi,* created around 1500, was sold at Christie's New York auction house for $450,312,500. This painting was the biggest art find in more than 100 years, and took 6 years to authenticate (Christies.com).

The sale of *Salvator Mundi* marked the highest price ever paid for a painting in auction. The painting was bought by a member of the Saudi royal family to be displayed in the new Louvre Museum in Abu Dhabi, United Arab Emirates, which opened in November, 2017. This sale surpasses Cézanne's *The Card Players* which sold in 2012 for $250,000,000.

I recently learned that the *Mona Lisa* had been insured for $100,000,000 in 1962. That value today would be $750,000,000.

I always wondered what priceless meant. I guess priceless now means $750,000,000 or $450,000,000.

MUSEUMS

The Michelangelo exhibit at the Metropolitan Museum of Art during the winter of 2017-18 was well worth seeing, if you could see it. The Met was so crowded that it resembled the subway at rush hour, and I was told that it had been like that for weeks.

Museum attendance is up, and I think that the recent sale of *Salvator Mundi* by da Vinci is part of the reason. I can't tell you how many people I corrected when they told me they were going to see the da Vinci exhibit, when they meant the Michelangelo exhibit.

Over my art teaching years, I convinced thousands of teenage and adult art students about the importance of visiting art museums. Now I laugh every time I see people flooding a museum. I ask myself, "Why did I do such a good teaching job? Now I can't see anything."

Natural Phenomena

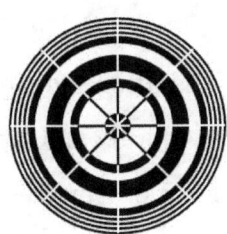

LIGHTNING

Across a huge expanse of night sky, three lightning bolts cascaded down in rhythmic time and equidistant, one, two, three. It was so well orchestrated that I thought it was a fireworks display.

This happened while I was stopped at a traffic light. I was driving from Westfield to Clark in central New Jersey, and I was so mesmerized by this cosmic display that I returned to reality only when honking cars urged me to move.

Since I had been a city dweller most of my life, my view was often blocked by tall buildings. The huge expanses of sky in Florida and New Jersey have always been a spectacular sight for me. But this particular incident was so unbelievable that it left a mark on my brain.

Every time there is a storm, I think, "Maybe I'll see that incredible sight again." But I probably never will!

HAIL

Once I was forced to exit the FDR Drive. The hail was so heavy, I was afraid my windshield would shatter. But never before or after did I experience what I experienced another time in Brooklyn.

During the week of New York State tests in February, my friend and I lunched and shopped on 86th Street, a busy shopping area in Brooklyn. We walked out of a store and could go no further–hail, the size of golf balls, was "raining from heaven." They looked like snow balls, but they were made of ice. They were so big and falling so fast, we could have gotten hurt if we had ventured out. That event lasted about 15 minutes.

I peeked out of the store, caught one and tried to preserve it, but by the time we returned to the school, it had melted. (And since there were no cell phones with cameras at that time, I have no pictures.)

MOON

This photograph tells its own story. The picture was taken in front of my friend's house in Westfield, NJ.

Photography by Judith Cohen

CLOUD

When my husband and I visited Venezuela, we stayed in La Guaira, the port of Caracas. A highlight of that trip was the Teleferico cable car up and down the almost 9,000-foot Avila Mountain from La Guaira to Caracas. The sight of Caracas from the air was spectacular, but more spectacular was the cloud that drifted in through one window and out the other. Did you ever feel a cloud? It was wet and icy. What a strange experience. My father had the same experience when he was in Venezuela. He claimed that he was "kissed by a cloud."

WINDY

When I first started exhibiting my paintings in the early 1970s, I exhibited in a cooperative art gallery, Gallery 99, on Atlantic Avenue in Brooklyn Heights.

When I visited the gallery, I often parked near the East River Brooklyn piers. There is a beautiful view of the Manhattan skyline there. Once, my six-year-old son and I were returning to our car which was parked near the water. A gust of wind literally swept my son off his feet. There was no storm, and no rain; in fact, it was a beautiful sunny day. This was an incident with no rhyme or reason as far as we were concerned.

There I was holding on to a tree. Where was my young son? I didn't see him but he was laughing. There he was on the ground, holding on to a fire hydrant. "Mommy, the wind blew me over." We both remember holding on to the tree and the fire hydrant for a long time. Finally we made a run for it.

I will never forget that bizarre incident.

A MISSED OPPORTUNITY

For nine years, my husband and I drove downtown to work on the FDR Drive. There it was–The World Trade Center–looming before us. It was a magnificent view and even more spectacular when the sun was rising between the two buildings.

Often, I said, "I must take a picture." It was before cell phones with cameras, so I never did take the picture. It was a real missed opportunity.

Recently, I looked on the internet and found the picture I would have taken. I'd like to share this experience with you. Log on to www.Pinterest.com, but you will have to search for the picture I would have taken.

ONE-HALF RAIN

In New York City, we marvel when it rains at Yankee Stadium in the Bronx and not in Manhattan. We do the same in New Jersey when it rains in Plainfield and not in Westfield, two towns away. But in Florida it's another story: you can be standing near someone, they are wet and you are dry.

In front of our condo building in Florida, the frontage being about 200 feet, a rain line was drawn at the 100-foot mark–on one side it was sunny, on the other side it was pouring. My friend opened her umbrella, not realizing that I was in sunshine.

Since this strange phenomenon lasted quite a while, we both had fun jumping in and out of the rain.

EARTHQUAKE IN BROOKLYN

A long time ago–I think in the early 1990s–we were asleep in our Brooklyn house. We awoke when our bedroom chandelier began to shake.

I told my husband, "It's a large truck outside that's causing the chandelier to shake." He retorted, "No, it's an earthquake."

It was an earthquake, we learned the following morning, approximately 3.5 on the Richter Scale. Until then, I did not know that there can be earthquakes in the eastern U.S. It turns out that seismic activity is rare, but does occur.

There have been larger earthquakes, such as the one in 2002 in Plattsburgh, NY with a 5.1 magnitude, and the one in Washington DC in 2011 with a magnitude of 5.8, which caused damage to the Washington Monument. My family was in Washington on the day of that earthquake; they were at the World War II Memorial. They felt it and tried to take a video, but didn't succeed. Recently, I watched a video of that earthquake on the internet.

SNOW STORIES

Snow can be beautiful, but leave it in a photograph or in a painting, not under foot.

But, snow stories are worth telling:

I remember December 1947, because 25.8 inches of snow fell in less than 24 hours, beating an 1888 record. I remember having a one-week snow vacation from school–New York City public schools were closed. My husband remembered that they couldn't open the front door of their Boro Park, Brooklyn house.

The largest snowstorms in the New York City area were in 1888, 1947, 1996, 2006 and 2010. The *New York Daily News* reported that the largest one was 26.9 inches in 2006. I was lucky; I missed that one. I was in Florida.

I never flew to or from Syracuse while in college because the small airlines that flew the Syracuse/New York route were unreliable. From my home in Brooklyn, I'd take the subway to Manhattan because my parents did not own a car, and the train from Grand Central Station to Syracuse. During a large snowstorm (probably the one in 1960), I had to return to school for exams. The subway from Brooklyn to Manhattan was very slow. Luckily, I made my train.

When I arrived in Syracuse five hours later, that widespread storm had dumped an amazing amount of snow. In town, where the train station was located, the city had cut narrow gaps in the huge piles of snow at the corners. I had to throw my suitcase over one of those snow mountains in order to hail a cab to take me to my dorm.

It was a very bad weekend to choose to go home!

In large snowstorms, cities–like New York City–do not know what to do with snow. In 1996, there was such a snow event that I still think about and laugh about.

One morning, there were large dump trucks stationed on every corner on the Upper East Side. These trucks had been borrowed from Buffalo to move snow to be dumped. In unison, snow shovels filled the trucks, and they "marched" in line to the East River to dump the snow.

The following morning, 1st Avenue between East 73rd Street and East 74th Street was closed to traffic. Overnight, the snow removers had built a snow mountain that stretched from East 73rd Street to East 74th Street on 1st Avenue that was as high as the four-story walk-ups on 1st Avenue. I'd never seen such a sight!

Driving home from work on the FDR Drive that afternoon, I saw the snow and ice that had been dumped in the East River. It looked like the calving ice floating near glaciers in Alaska. (Dumping snow in rivers creates another problem. Fish are killed by chemicals used to melt snow, but at the present time, there seems to be no better solution.)

When we arrived home, the snow mountain on 1st Avenue was gone. I guess that went into the East River too.

THE THREE-MILE RAINBOW

Once when we were in Florida, my husband and I saw an amazing rainbow. I've seen beautiful rainbows many times, but this one was just wide bands and kept going and going and going. It went on forever, perhaps to that "pot of gold."

We left from 100th Street, Bal Harbour, Florida and traveled along the ocean road to 163rd Street before turning west across a bridge over the Intracoastal Waterway. That rainbow kept going north.

I never saw and probably will never again see a phenomenon like this. It was truly mind-boggling and awe-inspiring.

THERE AND NOT THERE

As a Brooklyn resident, I watched the construction of the Verrazano Narrows Bridge connecting Brooklyn and Staten Island, which was completed in 1964.

Little did I know at that time, I'd eventually be teaching in a classroom with a view of that bridge. My classroom would have made a superb apartment. I was often distracted by that magnificent view.

The San Francisco Bay Bridge is sometimes photographed half in sun and half covered with clouds. Not the Verrazano. Never, in the 22 years that I taught in that art room, did I see a half-covered bridge. It was either there or not there, sometimes in sunshine, sometimes totally covered in clouds or fog.

Often students would pick up on this phenomenon. They'd say in amazement, "Mrs. Bard, where is the bridge?"

Photography by Sean Ramsey

WOW

The August 11, 2017 total solar eclipse was spectacular!

This was the first time in 99 years that a total solar eclipse passed through all of the U.S. It entered through Oregon and cut diagonally across the U.S. to South Carolina.

I saw the eclipse with my special glasses in New Jersey, so I didn't get to see the total eclipse, as pictured above, but I saw enough to say WOW. You can see photographs and videos on the internet.

Tragedies

9/11

My husband called me at 8:45 am to tell me that he saw a plane hit the north tower of the World Trade Center. He saw this from his office window. "We don't know what happened. I'm coming home (by car)." After that phone call, the phones and cell phones weren't working in lower Manhattan, so he couldn't reach me again. I did not see him until 12:30 when he knocked on our door. I'm sure you can imagine my anguish that morning. I was one of thousands who suffered on 9/11. I saw the first building fall on television in a firehouse on the Upper East Side. That firehouse lost 15 men at "Ground Zero."

The afternoon in Manhattan was almost as scary as the morning. Upper East Side residents roamed the streets, and everyone lined up at the blood donation center on East 67th Street. The center had so much blood donated that most, including us, were turned away.

And F-15s patrolled the sky!

Those F-15s scared me. For 14 years after 9/11, I cringed every time I heard a plane.

My doctor suggested using EMDR to help rid me of the plague. Eye Movement, Desensitization and Reprocessing (EMDR) is a form of psychotherapy developed by Francine Shapiro, PhD, that helps reduce the long-lasting effects of distressing memories and trauma. I had to concentrate on the plane that I saw as lights moved back and forth. Miraculously, on the second try, I saw the plane lift and fly away.

Believe it or not, I am no longer frightened by planes!

FLOOD

We talk about flooding and global warming now. In August of 1955, there were floods in the northeastern states that rank among the most destructive in United States history and were unprecedented at that time. Seventeen-inch rainfalls caused by Hurricane Diana impacted a large area from southeastern Pennsylvania to eastern Massachusetts.

I was at a Camp Fire Girls camp in Dingmans Ferry, Pennsylvania. We were on a mountain top so we were not affected by the flood, but we could not evacuate because of the devastation below. Even the road down the mountain had been washed out.

Helicopters flew by day and night. They certainly knew where we were. I remember that we covered several bunkhouse tops with white sheets on which we had written HELP in big, red letters. We had no electricity and no phone service. Thank goodness that we had many flashlights. The camp administration had no contact with the outside world. Our parents didn't know what happened to us when they heard about the flood on the news. My father told me later that he even thought about hiring a helicopter.

We were left stranded for at least five days, maybe a week. I remember that we were so busy that we didn't have time to contemplate the severity of our situation. We learned later that the Pennsylvania government knew we were safe and that we were not on their priority list.

I was one of the older campers there. Because the electricity was out, the water wasn't pumping to the taps. I was put in charge of the water-pail brigade bringing water from the nearby overflowing stream. All the water for bathing and cooking was boiled. It was a good thing that we had gas stoves!

The staff took good care of us and luckily we had sufficient food.

Finally, without warning, fire trucks arrived to evacuate us. We did not have much time to prepare for our leave, but we had packed most of our belongings days earlier.

The trip down the mountain on a fire truck was memorable. Our rescuers had made what is called a "corduroy road." They had laid logs side by side across the muddy, washed-out road in a pattern that looked like the fabric. I don't know how many days it took them to construct that.

Down below, there was true devastation everywhere. Houses were totally destroyed. In front of those that were still viable, owners had moved all of their furniture outside to dry. I particularly remember torn, wet mattresses. It must have really been some time we were atop that mountain because much of the water had receded. We were told that the whole area had been totally under water.

It had been a nightmare, but the ordeal was finally over. We returned to New York by bus. Needless to say, our parents were eagerly awaiting our arrival. We were so covered with mud that we all looked alike. Finally, my parents found me. I was happy to be home and safe, and I will never forget that I took three showers that night.

BLACKOUT

November 9, 1965 is famous as the largest power outage in the U.S. ever. The Great Northeast Blackout began in New York City during rush hour. I was eating dinner in my parents' apartment in Brooklyn Heights, overlooking the promenade with a view of the Manhattan skyline, when everything went black. I remember that amazing sight across the East River as buildings went dark, starting uptown and winding downtown.

My husband was at work in lower Manhattan. It was dangerous to drive, so he left his car and walked over the Brooklyn Bridge to Brooklyn Heights. We spent the night there. I spent much of that night on the promenade with reporters and photographers. What fun!

I did not go to work the following day–schools were closed and subways were not functioning. My husband walked back to work; I stayed in my parents' apartment.

Late in the afternoon, my husband and I drove home. I worried about the meat in the freezer and had a vision of ice cream dripping everywhere.

The irony of this story–the whole northeast went black, but not us. A small pocket in the Midwood section of Brooklyn was unaffected.

STARVING CHILDREN

My husband was a Holocaust survivor. Driven by the Nazis from his small town, Brok, in eastern Poland, he and his family were deported from Bialystok to a gulag in western Russia near the White Sea and then to Turkestan in Kazakhstan. He came to the United States with his mother in 1947, at age 11.

My husband and his family nearly starved for four years in Turkestan. If you had money, you could buy food, but his father had died from typhus soon after they arrived in Asia Minor. And there was no work for anyone. They had had some money when they arrived, but it had been used for doctor bills. His mother fried fish to sell "on the bazaar." That helped a bit, but most of the food the family had was scavenged.

As a child in the U.S. in the 1940s, my mother admonished me, "Please finish your food. Think of all the starving children in Europe."

Little did I know that I would marry one of those starving children.

The irony of this tragedy: there was something to eat. Large land turtles or tortoises roamed everywhere. The local people, primarily Uzbeks, had food to eat but never ate turtle. It was not because of dietary restrictions, but because my future husband's family just didn't know that turtle was edible.

CRASH

On December 16, 1960, a United Airlines DC-8 and a TWA Super Constellation collided over New York City.

According to the *New York Daily News* and *The New York Times*, one plane crashed in Park Slope, Brooklyn on 7th Avenue and Sterling Place. I only discovered this recently; all these years, had thought it had fallen on Flatbush Avenue, the main thoroughfare. The second plane fell on Miller Army Airfield in Staten Island.

Both planes came from the Midwest. One was headed for LaGuardia Airport, and the other for Idlewild Airport, which was later renamed John F. Kennedy Airport. With a total of 134 fatalities, on the planes and on the ground in Brooklyn, this was the worst airplane disaster in U.S. history up to that date (*The New York Times*, December 17, 1960).

I was in college at Syracuse University in upstate New York, but my parents were at home in Brooklyn, less than two miles from the crash site. I thought about debris that certainly could have fallen on my block or on my house.

These days, I think about the Williamsburgh Savings Bank on Flatbush and Atlantic Avenues. That bank building houses many dentists and that is where a dentist had pulled my wisdom teeth when I was a teenager. It was the tallest building in Brooklyn until 2009. Luckily, the plane that fell in Brooklyn did not hit that building which was very close to the crash site. This could have been a catastrophic disaster like 9/11.

New York Daily News, December 17, 1960
Photography by Hal Mathewson

I was frantic in Syracuse! The telephone lines were so congested that I couldn't reach my parents for three days. Thank goodness, they were okay.

This was a moment in U.S. airline history that few remember. For me it was significant. Not only was I concerned about my parents, but I later learned that I knew someone who was killed on one of those planes. He was coming home from the University of Michigan for the Christmas holiday.

ANTHRAX

After 9/11, I felt compelled to listen to the news even though I found it incredibly stressful. Also, since no cars were allowed in lower Manhattan for one month after 9/11, I was twice daily downtown near "Ground Zero" helping my disabled husband to and from work by subway.

There were lines of people holding flowers queuing on Broadway. For a month, I donned my medical mask and watched in sorrow. I still feel like crying when I see pictures of those lines.

One particular evening about one week after that terrible event, I was eating steak for dinner. I guess I didn't chew it very well and a piece caught in my gullet. The Heimlich Maneuver did not work, so I had to go to Lenox Hill Hospital.

The hospital took X-rays and then ordered an endoscopy to break up and push the meat down. I was ushered into a small room adjacent to the emergency room awaiting a gastroenterologist's arrival to perform the procedure. Soon after I was wheeled into the room, I was wheeled out again, replaced by someone else–two gurneys passing in the night. I was placed in a curtained cubicle in the emergency room where the endoscopy was successfully done.

But who was my mysterious replacement? I later learned that it was one of the patients who had died from inhaling anthrax powder. Of all the New York hospitals and all the possible times, this was quite the coincidence!

September 18, 2011, one week after 9/11, letters containing anthrax powder were mailed to several news media and congressional offices. Five people died from anthrax; the perpetrator or perpetrators were never found. Kathy Nguyen, an employee at Manhattan Eye and Ear Hospital, died at Lenox Hill Hospital on October 3, 2011. They are not sure how or where she was infected. She was the patient who had replaced me.

STORM AT SEA

My neighbor recently returned from crossing the Atlantic Ocean–Southampton to New York–on the Queen Mary II. That reminded me of this story:

Cunard Lines knew it was going to be a bad crossing, but they did not cancel our passage from Southampton to New York. In retrospect they should have, but 1956 was a different time. Now in 2017, a cruise line would have been sued by everyone on board for sailing in such bad weather. Looking back now, I think it is possible that we were on the northern edge of Hurricane Betsy.

I don't remember which ship we were on. My parents and I had taken either the Queen Mary I or the Queen Elizabeth I from New York to Southampton, then returned three weeks later on the other. But the passage home was certainly memorable.

Five days of storm! During that huge North Atlantic storm in early August of 1956, the captain turned the engine off and we rode the waves for at least three days.

Our cabin was front-ship; every time the ship hit the water, my stomach went down too. I can still feel it! Even I was seasick, and I am a good sailor. There were ropes strung everywhere, because you could only walk if you held on to them.

My father became sick on the first day, as most of the passengers did. He moaned and groaned in his bed. I was okay until the third day. Then I joined him in our cabin. My mother, always the sailor "par excellent," helped the crew, especially in the dining room. That rocking dining room was empty for three days, and I remember my mother trying to feed apples to the passengers who dared to enter.

Many of the crew became sick too, and I'm sure they never forgot that trip either. As a young teenager, after that grueling trip, I swore never to take a long ocean voyage again, and I never have.

However, I do cruise and have never had another bout with seasickness. In 2004, I took a Caribbean cruise with my husband on the Queen Mary II, considered her "maiden voyage" cruise year. I can now say that I've sailed on both the Queen Mary I and the Queen Mary II.

MY FIRST BOUT WITH TERRORISM

I spent ten weeks in France, most of that time at the University of Nancy in Alsace-Lorraine. This was a summer program jointly sponsored by Syracuse University and Notre Dame University.

By the end of the program, I was translating from French to English, and my French was fluent enough that the French students didn't believe I was an American. Because of my dark hair and eyes, they were sure I was either Spanish or Italian. Perhaps my descendants did originally come from that region.

When in Paris, I was enthralled with the ambiance and the museums, and felt comfortable with the French students and their families that I was fortunate to meet. I did not want to come home. My parents surprised me when they gave me permission to spend a year at the École des Arts Décoratifs, and Syracuse University was willing to give me credit since I was an art major.

I filled out applications, was interviewed at the French art school and looked for living space. My parents were preparing to send my art portfolio which was needed for final acceptance.

Then it happened! A bomb detonated close to the cold-water flat of the Sorbonne on the left bank where we were staying. It was the OAS, the Organization of Algerian States. This was 1961 and Algeria was continuing its struggle for independence, which was finally granted in 1962.

My parents heard about the bombing in Paris on the news. They called and informed me, "You are not staying in France." I responded, "That's okay; I'm terrified. I do not want to stay."

In October, two months after I had returned to the U.S., I read in a French newspaper that several Algerian demonstrators were drowned and were floating down the Seine. It was a difficult time in Paris.

I guess I made the right decision!

Transportation

RIGHT-HAND TURNS ONLY

My son took his car to the Brooklyn dealership about four miles from our home for a routine oil change and tire rotation.

When he was almost home after picking up the car, he called and said, "Ma, I can only make right-hand turns."

"Okay, that's interesting," I said. "Can you get home?"

He replied, "I think so," and he arrived a few minutes later, having made only right-hand turns. He was baffled and laughing.

The following morning, my husband accompanied my son back to the dealership, also making right turns only. Luckily, in this direction right-hand turns were in order.

At the dealership, up went the car, and down came the screwdriver which had been wedged in a position that made it impossible to make left-hand turns.

Mystery solved: the dealership apologized.

SANDWICHED

We were sandwiched on the Brooklyn Bridge. A car stopped short in the middle of the bridge, which created a ripple effect accident. Five cars were involved, holding traffic up for miles and hours. We were hit from behind and rammed into the car in front of us. Luckily, we were not hurt but just shaken.

Oh, for a cell phone. Few had them at that time, and I don't know how we lived without them.

My mother-in-law was waiting for us. We had no way to contact her for two hours until we were towed. She was "crazy" by the time we were able to call.

After that event, I bought my first "mobile" phone. It was housed in a suitcase with a zipper that I kept in the trunk of my car. It reminded me of a World War II walkie-talkie. It was large, but it worked.

The next day, a fellow teacher at work said, "We were in traffic for two hours yesterday; something happened on the Brooklyn Bridge." I responded, "I was the one responsible for keeping you in traffic for two hours."

PARKING IN MANHATTAN

Parking on the street in Manhattan is very difficult. It is more affordable than paying for a parking garage–especially when you have a NYC special disabled placard–but not without risk.

Our white car had interesting yellow streaks on it. When we took that car to Florida, people marveled at those strange decorations. They would ask, "What are those?" I would answer, "yellow New York taxicab marks." It was paint left behind when careless passengers would open the door. It seemed as if every time they did so, they would hit our car with the cab door.

The strangest experience was the morning I found the car covered with Chinese food. Only in Manhattan would something like that occur. Garbage trucks are allowed to collect garbage only at night. The nightly beep, beep of the backup warning signal is a Manhattan phenomenon. Because the restaurants have to use private sanitation trucks, and there are so many restaurants bunched together, the noise goes on steadily.

I suppose the men on the truck picking up garbage from the Chinese restaurant must have had bad aim. Luckily, Kentucky Fried Chicken on the corner had a water spigot outside, and the kind workers washed the car for me. They couldn't get the grease off, however. Four trips to the car wash barely touched that grease. We didn't know what to do.

Our daughter-in-law finally suggested using dishwasher liquid. I can vouch for dishwashing liquid on dishes–it also cleans cars. That finally did the trick!

THE MISSING CAR

One week, thieves took the hub caps; the next week they took the car. I walked around the neighborhood for hours, thinking that maybe I had parked in another location, before I reported the missing car to the police.

My father was visiting from Florida. This was the first time I would have been able to take him to the airport. It was a weekend, so I was not working. But no car!

Our car had been parked on 2nd Avenue in front of a superette. The owner used to babysit our car when it was parked there. I don't know why, but he used to tell me that he did. He said the car was there that morning when he came to work early, so it wasn't taken at night, which we had suspected.

It was a long time before I figured this out. There was a parade that day on 5th Avenue. Parking was permitted on the east side of 2nd Avenue where I was parked. The city towed cars parked on the west side of 2nd Avenue. Some savvy thief must have known of the towing program and had taken advantage of the situation to tow my car. I guess no one questioned this. The police made us check with the city before pronouncing that the car was stolen.

Insurance paid quickly and we bought a new car. A month later, we received a phone call from a garage in Yonkers. "You have to pay a storage fee if you want to store your car here."

My husband told him our story and said that we didn't want the car. He also asked the condition of the car. "It's fine, except that it's missing seats," said the garage man. Then, we realized what had happened: first, the thief filled an order for hub caps, then for seats.

The garage didn't want the car either. "What am I going to do with it?" said the garage man. My husband said, "You can use it for parts, or better, steal some seats and sell it."

MORE CAR STORIES

How many times have you tried to open the wrong car? To me, all gray cars look alike, and I've done that too many times. Once I was interrupted by a laughing owner.

Recently, I did something even funnier. I entered an identical-looking gray car that was parked in front of mine. I pride myself on how neat I keep my car, and obviously this owner did also, so there were no telltale signs. The transponder worked; I got in, I put the key in the ignition, and it fit. But the car would not start. I said to myself out loud, "Oh no, the starter."

Then I looked down at the steering wheel and realized that the car was the same make but a different division of that automobile company.

If the car had started, I would have driven away in the wrong car! I thought, "Next time I had better buy a car of a different color."

The story has another chapter, though. I did buy another gray car. I got a good deal on a new car with all the safety devices.

New cars take some "getting used to." They beep when another car is too close, even when you are motionless in a parking lot. They divert accidents by self-braking which is scary if you are used to an older model car. They are keyless and after six months, I was still reaching for car keys in my pocketbook. Some can also drive themselves, but I'm definitely not ready for that.

And they talk when the GPS is not engaged. One day, my friend's husband drove five of us to a concert in his new SUV. He knew the way, so the GPS was not on. A police car was blocking one of the roadways and we needed to detour. As he tried to decide which of many potential routes to our destination he should take, he hesitated for a moment. Suddenly, we thought there was a sixth passenger in the car. A voice said, "Are you having trouble; may I help you?"

Another friend drove her new car for two hours–the longest trip she had taken in this new vehicle. After the two-hour drive, alone in the car, someone said, "I think you need a cup of coffee."

New cars are safer, but they are also making us laugh.

THE GPS

We pulled up in front of the hotel in West Orange, New Jersey where we were attending a wedding.

The GPS said, "You're eight miles from your destination."

My husband looked at me–"Maybe we're at the wrong hotel?" he suggested.

It was the GPS that was wrong, however. We were in the right place.

On another occasion, my son was driving the family from Queens to Woodmere, Long Island, which is not a long drive. There was construction, a detour and beach traffic. The GPS, trying to navigate and find a feasible route, got lost. First, she said we should turn right, then changed that to turning left. That left turn would have put us on the exit ramp of the Jackie Robinson Parkway heading into oncoming traffic. We turned off the GPS.

I had to find out why the GPS can be so inaccurate, and discovered by researching this that the Global Positioning System (GPS) was developed by the United States Department of Defense. They allow civilians to use the system, but there are limitations: a GPS is only accurate within 13 feet of the receiving GPS device. As a result, a GPS may get confused when it cannot discern between two very close roads, or when it thinks you have yet to turn a corner even though you did. This is what we have to live with to ensure military security. It's too bad that we do not have access to the complete system.

Since I find the GPS to be so frustrating, I prefer to pull computer directions for new destinations. But the GPS is certainly helpful when you are lost.

AND HOW DID YOU GET HERE?

Our favorite Florida restaurant was in Islamorada in the Keys. Every time we journeyed from Miami to dinner there, we were greeted at 5:00 pm by a blue heron waiting for his dinner near the kitchen door.

On one occasion, my husband overheard a conversation. The waitress asked the people, "How did you get here today?" The answer was, "By helicopter, of course." My husband ignored what he had heard.

When we left, lo and behold–a bright blue helicopter was parked two spots away from our car in the restaurant's parking lot.

CHEAP DATE

A cheap date was to drive to Kennedy Airport, sit on the shoulder of Rockaway Parkway and watch planes land. The touchdown on the runway was right over a fence where we were standing. The plane's wheels were already down, the plane was very low and very big.

So exciting! I still love it!

AIR TRAFFIC CONTROLLER STRIKE

On August 5, 1981, President Ronald Reagan fired all the air traffic controllers in the U.S. They had been on strike and in consequence, 7,000 flights had been cancelled on August 3, 1981. Based on a 1955 law which was reconfirmed in 1971 by the Supreme Court, President Reagan deemed this strike illegal (Wikipedia). The government expected real problems, but airline supervisors and the military pitched in and air service was restored quickly.

We were returning from a vacation in St. Croix, Haiti and Jamaica that August. Our return flight from St. Croix should have taken approximately three hours, but took six because we were circling. As we went round and round, the pilot would announced, "We are now flying over scenic Deer Park, Long Island… we are now flying over beautiful Canarsie, Brooklyn… " and so on. After three hours of circling, the pilot announced, "We have clearance for landing; we are running out of fuel."

ISLAND HOPPING

We were island-hopping in the Caribbean in the 1960s on Air France jets. On one hop, you must get fed, so the airline said. That turned out to be from St. Croix to Haiti. But who expected a gourmet three-course meal in less than a half hour. That's what happened. We were served on the way up and were still eating as we landed. They had to wait for us to finish before we could deplane.

This was one of the best meals I've had in my life, but I don't remember what I ate. Too bad it was so rushed. Not only were we eating fast, but laughing all the time. How did they do this? They did! Everyone was very, very busy!

UNSCHEDULED

Long ago, before cockpits were locked, I flew in the cockpit of a new DC-9 from Acapulco to Merida, which is the capital of Yucatan, with an unscheduled stop in Oaxaca. The airline had called us–the flight was leaving one day early. Because this scheduled flight became unscheduled, there were very few passengers, so the pilot invited me into the cockpit. The panoramic view was spectacular.

MIAMI TO FORT LAUDERDALE

Our plane from the Caribbean was supposed to land in Fort Lauderdale, but instead we ended up in Miami International Airport. This was very inconvenient, since my father was waiting in Fort Lauderdale. Many of the passengers had similar problems, and we all bombarded the crew with questions.

"Be patient," the stewardess said, "we'll be in Fort Lauderdale soon." Sure enough, the 747 took off, flew 30 land miles, and 5 minutes later it landed in Fort Lauderdale. We, of course, asked why the plane made two Miami stops that time, but didn't get an answer.

Now I know why it happened. On another trip, I recently met a retired Delta Airline pilot. I asked him why we stopped in both places. He told me that when airports are busy, the planes frequently stop at both Miami and Fort Lauderdale airports. Passengers are allowed to get off in Miami, but new ones may not embark. After that, the plane would take off, gain a cruising altitude of 4,000 feet, and fly for two to three minutes at that height before descending and landing.

Mystery solved!

NO JET LAG

In 1978, on one of many trips to Israel, I took my 12-year-old niece to keep my son, aged 8, company.

We arrived at Kennedy Airport and checked in as usual. But before boarding, my niece and I were ushered by El Al Airline into a special room where we were told to undress down to our underwear. My husband and son waited for us, wondering what was transpiring. El Al, which was always extremely security conscious, was obviously looking for something a woman could hide–they must have had a tip.

The flight was as strange as the check-in experience. We had four seats in the center of a Boeing 747. The children were slumping over and slept on top of me. For all intents and purposes, I had no seat on a full flight.

The Israeli basketball team was on board–lots of big tall men. The stewardesses put wooden boards across aisles in some sections, so they could stretch their legs. I found such a seat until I needed the lady's room. I returned and found that even my board seat was had been taken by someone, so I sat on the floor in an empty corner. Then there was an emergency–someone needed oxygen. Where do you think they brought her? I don't think I sat for more than one hour during that 11-hour flight. I certainly did not sleep on that whole night flight.

When we arrived in Tel Aviv, our cousins took us to their kibbutz, Maale Hahamisha, in the Judean Hills. My husband's cousin was one of the founders of that kibbutz in 1938. Everyone was exhausted but me! Everybody took a nap but me! I lost that day. I had no jet lag, and I proceeded functioning as usual like I had slept the night.

This was the strangest time-related incident I have ever experienced.

ANOTHER AIRLINE ANTIC

When my husband and I arrived at Miami Airport a few years ago, we needed to return our rental car. Unfortunately, construction prevented us from following the marked route to the return lot. What to do?

I noticed a van picking people up that was marked with the logo of "our" rental company, and I said to my husband, "Quick, follow that van." We followed it through the maze of roads in that huge airport. It was a very convoluted drive that took at least 20 minutes and I have no idea where we went, but I was right. We finally arrived at the correct place to return our car. Thank goodness we came to the airport early.

ONCE AROUND THE ARC DE TRIOMPHE

A long time ago, I rode on the back of a motorcycle in Paris. Once around the Arc de Triomphe was one time too many for me.

"Let me off," I cried. The only thing I could think of was "a body in motion tends to stay in motion."

Then, one of my students fell off the back of a motorcycle near the school where I taught. She was decapitated. Since she was an art student, I had to return her artwork to her parents. That was a terrible experience. And that was the end of motorcycles for me!

My son's friend was talking about buying a motorcycle. When I heard this, I said to my son, "Don't you dare ride on his motorcycle. If you get hurt in a ski accident (he is a trained skier), I'll be at the hospital before you. If you get hurt falling off a motorcycle, don't call home."

NEW YORK CITY SUBWAY STORIES

The first time I was on the 65th Street station of the #1 train which runs under Broadway, I noticed a strange sight: most of the people on the platform had a finger in each ear. I couldn't imagine why. I later learned that they were Julliard music students protecting their hearing.

I did a reverse commute by subway from Manhattan to Brooklyn when I took a college adviser's job in a private high school. I'd ride in the center car where there was always a policeman or a train engineer. I just felt safer because there were so few people on the train doing a reverse commute in rush hour. After 9/11, the policeman was replaced by a military man with an Uzi in hand.

The D train (the Brighton Line) and the B train (the West End Line) are approximately three miles apart in Brooklyn. Suddenly, the B became the D and the D became the B. What confusion! I marveled. That not-so-brilliant decision had to have been made by a non-New Yorker.

When I was a child there was a sign in every subway car: "Please extinguish the illumination. Please do not expectorate." I wonder how many people understood what that meant.

When I was an art student, I used to carry four-foot by five-foot paintings on the bus and subway going home from Pratt Institute. How I did that is now beyond my comprehension. I also looked like an artwork myself–covered with paint. That part people couldn't see since we were so crammed together.

Travel

IT'S A SMALL WORLD

My friend was visiting Rome. She entered her hotel, opened the door and walked into the lobby. There was her aunt sitting near the entrance–an aunt she spoke to on the phone, but hadn't seen in years.

My friend asked, *"What are you doing here?"*

Her aunt responded, *"What are you doing here?"*

My friend lives in New Jersey; her aunt lives in California.

I had a similar experience when my husband and I were vacationing in Bermuda. We stayed at a hotel on a cliff where you got to the tenth floor by going down instead of up. The elevator door opened on the eighth floor. Standing there were our niece and nephew.

"What are you doing here?"

"What are you doing here?"

We lived in Brooklyn; they lived in New Jersey. We saw them often, but we didn't know about their impending Bermuda trip.

It's a very small world!

SEA OF GALILEE

My husband and I visited Israel the summer of 1966, just a year before the Six Day War in the Middle East. My husband's Israeli cousin seems to have taken us to every dangerous spot in the country.

"Watch out for pot shots here," he'd say in Golan and in other high places.

The day before our scheduled trip to Galilee, we heard there had been an aerial dog fight over the Sea of Galilee. But no one on the news said that people should avoid going there, so off we went. Never did we expect to see what we saw: a Russian MIG crashed in the middle of the lake with one wing protruding high above the water. That was some view for our luncheon of St. Peter's fish (tilapia) in a small lakeside restaurant.

I wish I still had the pictures, but they were lost in our move from Manhattan to New Jersey.

Photography by Nancy Goodman

NOTRE DAME

It turns out that my French is just as good as I thought it was. My cousin and my friend accompanied me to France in 1987. They have been kidding me ever since that I led them up the wrong path because of bad French, but they were wrong.

Le tour in French means the tour, *la tour* means the tower, *tours* or *les tours* can mean either based on context.

The three of us arrived at the rear of Notre Dame Cathedral. There was a large sign "TOURS," and lots of tour buses and several long lines of people. Assuming these were the lines for tour groups, or for cathedral tours, and since we had purchased week-long museum passes, we deemed there was no need for us to wait on line. We proceeded to the front of the lines. We were ushered into the cathedral and directed to a staircase, a very long spiral one. We questioned where we were but continued on. Up, up, up. My cousin snidely commented that she just bumped into Quasimodo coming down the stairs.

That was the best made mistake, but it was not because of my "bad French." The sign was really confusing. We finally arrived at the top. The view of Paris was unbelievable and we were up close and personal with wonderful gargoyles. We could have climbed higher on an outside metal ladder. I guess that led to a tower, but we had enough climbing for that day and were awed enough by our mistake excursion.

This was a wonderful trip. I particularly remember our camaraderie. We visited seven museums in Paris in five days. I also vividly remember the Loire Valley and Carcassonne from that trip. And of course, I still laugh every time I think of *TOURS.*

ST. GOTTHARD'S PASS

My first trip to Europe was with my parents, in 1956, on a three-week whirlwind tour.

The most memorable part of that tour was our climb and descent through the St. Gotthard's Pass in southern Switzerland–99 hairpin turns. As I counted, I drew the turns in my sketchbook. There really were 99. The bus was specially equipped with setback wheels, and the front of the bus hung over the edge of the mountain road. It was very scary and some people didn't feel well. But it was breathtaking, and of course, there was snow in the pass in July.

When my husband and I traveled to Italy many years later, we flew home from Zurich, Switzerland. Once again, we would be going through the St. Gotthard's Pass from Italy to Switzerland. I was excited and raved to everyone on that tour what they could expect. Surprise! Apparently, you can still make those 99 hairpin turns through the pass, but we took the new and faster route through a 10-mile tunnel which was completed in 1980.

I hadn't meant to build up everyone's hopes for nothing. They were all angry at me because they didn't get to see those spectacular turns and views.

Eventually, even that 10-mile tunnel was insufficient. In 2016, a 35-mile tunnel was completed to ease the traffic between central Europe and Italy.

MONTE CARLO

On that same European trip when I was 14 years old, I made a collection of coins and toilet paper. My father drilled holes in the coins and I made a bracelet. And the toilet paper ended up in a scrap book, which I kept and showed to friends and family for a long time. I'm sure I still have it in a box buried in my basement storage compartment.

It was quite a collection of toilet paper: some samples were like sandpaper, some were like wax paper; others were very thin or very thick and coarse like paper toweling. None looked like what we call toilet paper.

The best example was in Monte Carlo. Now there is a large underground parking facility, but in those days all the tour buses parked in front of the Prince's Palace. There was a portable toilet in the parking lot for tourist use. The toilet paper in there was *The New York Times,* cut up.

LOST IN THE CATACOMBS

Beginning in the 2nd century AD, Christians began to bury their dead in underground chambers beneath Rome. *Wikipedia* says that Christians, believing in the Second Coming, preferred burial to the usual Roman practice of cremation. I also discovered that there are at least 40 catacombs beneath Rome, many of them found recently.

Underground, the frescoes, sculptures and gold medallions make these chambers a museum of early Christian art. I remember the artwork vividly, but I was particularly taken with the bones and skulls, many being children's bones.

I found this tour to be fascinating but very creepy, especially when we got lost. Apparently, our guide didn't speak a word of English, but memorized his explanations. He did not tell us that there was a fork in those sometimes very narrow passages. It was a large group, and how many of us took the wrong fork, I do not know. It was dark and we were wandering around unable to find our way out. Eventually, the Catacombs administration realized that we were missing.

They rescued us from that winding maze of underground passages.

ALASKA

On my most recent cruise, I saw 4,000 miles of snow-covered mountains with waterfalls, fjords, glaciers and wonderful animals. Alaska is a very special place.

I called Alaska Airlines to make reservations from Anchorage to Vancouver. I was told that it was a non-stop three-hour flight.

I said, "The flight from New York to Miami is only two and one-quarter hours."

It turns out that from Anchorage to Vancouver is 2,100 miles. That's when I realized the expanse of Alaska. What was once called "Seward's Folly," (the 1867 purchase of Alaska from Russia for 7.2 million dollars by then Secretary of State William Seward) is a tremendous swath of land. Alaska is one-fifth the size of the entire lower 48 states and bigger than Texas, California and Montana combined.

After much consideration, my friend and I decided to take a two-week round-trip cruise, starting and ending in Seattle. We went north to Kodiak Island, home of the large Kodiak bears, where most cruises do not venture. It was June, but we wore raincoats over our winter parkas. Some passages were still blocked with ice.

The ocean throughout the trip was aqua, just as it is in the Caribbean. I had thought all water north of New York was gray. That was a real discovery for me. Also, I had never seen so much daylight in 24 hours. Sunset was at 11:30 pm and sunrise at 3:30 am. It never got really dark. On a cloudy day, the glaciers appeared blue because the dense glacier ice absorbs all the other colors of the spectrum except blue, which we see.

Photography by Millicent McKinley

We saw bears, Dall sheep, sea otters, moose, whales, wolves, elk, salmon and eagles. They were all quite as amazing as I had expected.

There is something compelling about Alaska. Whether it is the enormity, the pristine beauty, the serenity, the quietness or all of the above, I felt a religious sense of awe. I still see those snow-covered mountains running before my eyes.

When I first heard that many passengers on this cruise had taken the exact trip three or four times, I was baffled. I now understand. I am ready to return.

ANIMAL STORIES

WHY WE GOT A DOG

My husband brought home four strays. I don't know whether they found him or he found them. I'm a dog lover, but I didn't want any of them. We were both working and I was going to school at night. We had the room, but no time for a dog. We took each of these strays to a local pet shop. The owner gave them shots and found them homes.

The story of the fifth stray follows:

I was in my classroom, teaching. My supervisor entered the room and said, "Call your husband. He wants you to pick up the dog." This was before cell phones, so the call had come to the school office.

I responded, "What dog?"

My husband's story:

"As I got on the subway this morning, a young Weimaraner came running onto the train. People were terrified, so I took off my belt to use as a leash, got into a cab, and he is now in the garage at my mother's house. Please pick up the dog after work and bring him home."

This puppy was too nice to give to the pet store. We took an ad in the *New York Post*. We received a phone call from the owner of the dog. We returned him.

Six months later, we received a call from the dog's owner– "We're getting a divorce; do you want the dog?" I wasn't sure, so we took him for a week trial. By that time, he was one year old and too strong for me to handle, so we returned him again.

At that point, I said to my husband, "If you bring another stray home, you'll have to choose between the dog and me."

Shadow
Photography by Arthur Bard

We spent a weekend at a hotel in Connecticut. In *The New York Times,* we saw a breeder's ad for Gordon setter puppies. We decided to take a look. Seven beautiful puppies were in a round enclosure. The breeder opened the gate and our dog sat on my husband's shoe. SOLD! He immediately came home with us. We bought him in Trumbull, Connecticut, which from then on, we dubbed "Trouble Connecticut." Problem solved–no more strays.

This is not the end of the story. We had the dog for 13 years before he passed away.

Now my husband started bringing home stray cats. At least they lived outside, since I'm allergic to cats. At one point, we had seven grown cats and more kittens than I could count. I was often carrying 30 cans of cat food home from the local supermarket. One day, I accidentally ran over and killed a kitten. I was so upset that I cried the whole day.

"That's it," I said, "you choose between the cats and me!"

Again this is not the end of the story. I recently learned more stories about my husband's dogs and cats from my sister-in-law. I knew that he had dogs in Europe and Asia Minor during World War II. These animals were his friends; they brought him comfort in times of great stress. What he never told me about were the cats he hid in the basement of their Brooklyn home after they immigrated to America. It took some time before my future mother-in-law figured out how these animals came into their basement.

What an animal lover!

SMART DOG

Our dog, a 72-pound Gordon setter, hated cars, baths and the doctor.

He was smart and cunning. When he was an eight-week-old puppy, he plopped his water bowl in my lap. Big enough to sit on the couch person-style, he did so with a leg crossed. If we had visitors, he joined the company on the couch, and seemed to understand everything that was said. Sometimes he participated in the conversation with gestures and grunts. If he had the right kind of vocal chords he would have spoken English, but he certainly spoke "dog."

But how did he know we were about to leave for the veterinarian's office? I didn't talk about our impending visit and went out of my way to act like we were going to visit family or friends.

I never discovered how he sensed where we were going, but I certainly remember always having to pick up and put that 72-pound dog in the car.

I conclude–dogs have more than a keen sense of smell.

DOG THIEF

I came home from work; everything looked okay. Upstairs, however, something was strange–a big circle of "stuff" in the middle of the master bedroom floor.

"Oh no," I thought, "not another robbery."

We owned a house in Brooklyn for 27 years. During that time, we had two robberies that I would describe as "bad." But this time, when I looked more closely, I realized that there were only shoes in that perfect circle. Nothing else had been moved or taken. This was a very strange robbery.

I pondered, "What could this be?" Suddenly, I had a thought. "Could it be the dog?" He was not allowed upstairs because of allergy problems, and to my knowledge he had never gone upstairs. But as he got older, he became more brazen.

I did some research. Dogs do make nests. He must have made a nest, a perfect circle to fit his size.

We determined that we needed a gate on the staircase. Thank goodness this wasn't another robbery, but why didn't I take a picture?

BLOODHOUND

Every year, we attended the Westminster Kennel Club Dog Show at Madison Square Garden. Our own dog was a Gordon setter, so we were especially interested in Gordon setters.

One year, I could not attend; my husband went by himself after work. He came home very late. Since there were no cell phones in those days, he hadn't called.

I asked him, when he finally arrived, "Where were you?"

"I couldn't leave," he responded.

Then he told me his story:

"I was walking around the large room where the dogs stay when not in competition. The large dogs sit on pillows or blankets–they are not caged. There was this beautiful bloodhound with floppy ears and big sad eyes. He was lying there quietly by himself. I did not know where his master was. I petted him and spoke to him. Then I tried to leave. He started howling pathetically. When I spoke to him he quieted down, but the minute I started to leave, he began howling again. I waited for the owner to return–that took over an hour. He had gone to dinner."

When the owner finally returned he asked me, "Why are you sitting here?"

I told him what had occurred. "He's such a big baby," said the owner. "And he is smart as well. He got you."

LLAMA

You think this love affair was only with dogs? Once, in the Miami Zoo, my husband fell in love with a llama whose head projected way above the fenced in area where it stayed. I admit the animal was beautiful, with big blue eyes. My son and I left him there and walked around the zoo. We returned to find the llama's head resting on my husband's shoulder. We had trouble pulling them apart. "Time to leave."

Molting Dall Sheep on Trans-Canada Highway
Photography by Arthur Bard

CANADIAN STORIES

TUNNEL

On the Trans-Canada Highway, we were backed up in traffic for more than two hours. When we finally got near the source of the tie-up, we discovered that it had been caused by a by a bear and Dall sheep. The bear was now on the side of the road. Police had been directing traffic, but there were still sheep crossing the road.

The Canadian government, in order to alleviate this problem, was in the process of constructing tunnels under the highway so the animals could pass. I thought this was a "cool" idea, and I'm sure that it has helped.

SQUIRREL, OH MY!

When my husband and I were on tour in western Canada, we befriended an Australian family with a teenage daughter.

How excited that girl was when she saw a squirrel for the first time!

I thought, "It's like an American seeing a kangaroo in the wild for the first time in Australia." That just proves how similar people are around the globe.

BANFF

The herd of moose rented the gas station in town every night, so it seemed. When the owner turned the lights off at 6:00 pm, the moose miraculously appeared, and when he turned the lights on at 6:00 am, they disappeared.

We saw this spectacle for several days. This was certainly a mutual admiration society.

LAKE LOUISE

We arrived at Lake Louise. I was so excited that I was going to swim in that beautiful lake.

I told the bellhop, as we followed him with our bags to the room, that I planned to quickly don my bathing suit and go for a swim. I asked if there were fish in the lake. He never answered my question. Instead, he belted out, "You can't swim in that lake, it's a glacier lake. You need a special suit or you'll get hypothermia." I was disappointed, but spent most of that day and night on our balcony looking at that spectacular view. Lake Louise is truly one of the most beautiful places I've ever been.

ANOTHER SQUIRREL STORY

Squirrels can look quite cute at times, but oh can they be destructive.

The cat finally chased the squirrel out! We didn't know how that bushy-tailed pest got in–perhaps through a hole in the roof of my friend's Brooklyn home. Her husband hid. My friend ran around with a coat over her head, and I was outside listening to everyone scream. That squirrel was in every room in the house, causing destruction everywhere it went. Finally, her big orange cat got in the act and chased the squirrel out through the open front door. Out and gone, thank goodness! I never forgot that incident.

This story is true; however, two days after I had written it, I realized that I hadn't been there. I had heard this story so many times that I guess I must have dreamed that I had been standing outside witnessing the incident. Memories can be strange and sometimes can be wrong.

CHICKEN SALAD

In an art camp I attended in Connecticut, we had a large animal farm. Why I was chosen to visit a farmer and return with a dozen baby chicks, I don't know, but I was. Off we went in a panel truck and returned with the cutest yellow furry balls.

I visited and played with "my pets" as they grew. By the end of the summer they were quite large. I never gave a thought to where these chickens or for that matter all the animals (including a cow that had given birth in the middle of the night) would go when camp closed.

On the last day of camp, we hosted a festival for family and friends. It was a time to say goodbye and many campers left with family that day. We had a feast that featured chicken salad. Later, I discovered that I had eaten my pet chickens.

To this day, I can tolerate chicken, but I can't eat chicken salad!

A SEA OF WHITE

In one school where I taught, classes were in session but I had no class. I was busy at work in my room on the fourth floor and decided to walk down the stairs to my office on the first floor. Windows were located on each landing of the staircase revealing the football field below. It was a sea of white birds. There must have been thousands. They were not gulls or Canada geese, but they were large and they covered the football field. I searched in bird books and on the internet, but never did discover their species.

I don't know how long they had been stationed on the field, but while I was transfixed, they took off. It looked like a huge pillow fight as they headed south. It was the largest migration I ever witnessed.

I asked my students and the teachers if they had seen the birds on the field. "No, no, no, no."

I think I was the only one who captured that extraordinary spectacle.

INTELLIGENT BIRDS

On a trip to Gloucester, Massachusetts, we came upon a flock of very smart seagulls. As they scrounged for food, they never fought each other for a morsel, as gulls usually do. Instead, they lined up atop a fishery and dove into the water one at a time to retrieve discarded fish entrails. Then each flew to the back of the line and awaited its turn again.

We watched for more than an hour, so intrigued. Henry Ford invented the assembly line. What should we say about these intelligent birds?

PICK UP YOUR SHOES

"Pick up your shoes, pick up your shoes," screeched my blue parakeet. (He should still be telling me that. I tripped over my slippers the other day.) My mother patiently taught him to say about 20 words. In most other ways, he acted more like a dog than a parakeet. That bird would watch television on my shoulder, take a bath under the kitchen sink faucet, and sit on the piano with head cocked and listen to me practice. He even chewed up my homework one day which my teacher didn't believe.

Of course, when my cousin unexpectedly visited, that was another matter. She was terrified of anything that flew. Once she chased him and he flew into the refrigerator. She slammed the door shut. Luckily, we saw what happened, laughed and immediately freed him. My cousin remembers this story differently: she remembers accidentally hitting me in the mouth while dodging the flying bird. I had braces at the time and needed a trip to the orthodontist. Perhaps there were two episodes.

The usual life span of a parakeet like this is five to ten years. Ours died after three years. We decided to bury him in a shoebox in the garden in front of our apartment house. It was dark. We were so upset, we buried the flashlight as well.

Photography by Joellen Bard

WHERE DO THEY GO?

Every day at approximately noon, a dozen pelicans would take off in V formation from fir trees in Haulover Park which is at 102nd Street on the ocean just north of Bal Harbour, Florida. Their destination: somewhere to the south. At four pm, the flock would return.

We often all sat at our condominium's pool wondering where they went. We laughed when we thought of hiring a helicopter to follow them.

We never learned where they went, but it was a daily conversation for years. We sat and waited for them–they never failed us.

MY FIRST MEMORIES

My first memory comes from when I was two years old–hard to believe but true. I had a terrible case of chicken pox, and I remember sitting in my crib scratching while my grandmother sat and watched.

My second memory is from the summer when I was three. My family vacationed at Lake Winnipesaukee in New Hampshire. I have many photos, little me with a golf club on a beautiful lush green golf course. And I never forgot the boxer who bounded into our car when we arrived. I was scared to death, but that experience never stopped me from being an animal lover.

I clearly remember being stung by a bee on the eyelid, while I was playing with other children on that golf course. We must have disturbed a beehive because we were all bitten, some so seriously that they were taken to the hospital. I was the lucky one with only one bite. Couldn't that bee have found a better place to bite me than on my eyelid?

Most memorable from that summer were walks on the golf course with my father. I would swear that I saw a huge rabbit. Now I assume I was so tiny that a rabbit appeared very large to me.

To this day when I see a rabbit on our lawn in New Jersey, I'm reminded of New Hampshire and have a vision of that large rabbit.

SNAKES

I am petrified of snakes–I guess that goes back to my childhood. I was in upstate New York at my aunt and uncle's summer home. They had a rock garden, and one day a long, black snake (probably a garter snake) was entwined around the rocks. I stood there petrified–perhaps a minute, perhaps an hour. Eventually, I ran!

I didn't want my son to be afraid of snakes, so I sheepishly petted a boa at the Miami Science Museum. I guess I succeeded–he is not afraid of snakes.

CHIMPANZEES

ZIPPY

While I was browsing the internet recently, I watched Zippy the chimpanzee roller-skating on the *Ed Sullivan Show*. Long ago, I used to see a chimp roller-skating in the hall of my aunt's Manhattan co-op building. I think this was Zippy, because I remember seeing him on television at the time. His master would leave the door to his apartment open, and the chimp would skate without supervision for hours. I remember that he wore a T-shirt and a diaper. Oh, was that fun to watch! You can watch Zippy skate on the internet too.

MIAMI ZOO

At the Miami zoo, I really saw the differences in animal personalities.

The zookeeper was feeding the chimpanzees, and they put on a show for us. He threw an apple to each chimp. You could see which chimp was right-handed, which one was left-handed, and which one could have been a baseball player. There was one large female. She was lazy or smart–she let the apple drop and then picked it up. As we stood and watched this funny spectacle, in the background appeared a young chimp carrying another chimp on his back. We asked the zookeeper what that chimp was doing. His answer was, "They know when they need help. That young chimp is helping an elderly chimp who can no longer walk."

Photography by Joellen Bard

MOVING ROCK

On a long forest hike in camp in Pennsylvania, our group stopped to rest. I stood on a large rock or, at least, I thought it was a rock. Then it moved. I quickly jumped off. Everyone laughed when we realized that I'd been standing on a large land turtle. No, rocks don't move!

TURTLE WALK

I was crossing a typical small Brooklyn street early one morning when I saw something that made me stop dead to watch. Two cars near the intersection also stopped.

An elderly Chinese man, I think the grandfather, and a young boy were crossing the street. The boy was walking an approximately eight-inch green and brown turtle on a rope leash. We were all so astonished we could not move, but patiently waited until the boy, his grandfather and the turtle finished their crossing.

On July 8, 2017, I heard a newsflash about more turtles. Five hundred turtles were saved from the tarmac at John F. Kennedy Airport, which is located on the side of Jamaica Bay. According to NBC Channel 4 News in New York, travelers said, "This was the cutest reason for a delay."

THE FISH IN THE BATHTUB

When our son was young, we found a book called *The Carp in the Bathtub* (Barbara Cohen, Kar-Ben Publishing, 1972).

Then my husband told his story: "My mother used to buy a large live carp. She would let it swim in the bathtub until she was ready to make gefilte fish. I didn't want her to kill the fish, so I used to lock myself in the bathroom with the fish. It took hours to convince me to come out."

That was exactly the story in the book. I guess my husband wasn't the only animal-loving child.

THE BUTTERFLY GIRL

I know many people who dislike flying things: bugs, butterflies and birds. Never did I know anyone who loved them until we visited Butterfly World in Coconut Creek, Florida. As my husband and I and our friends were walking, we noticed something unique. A seven-year-old girl was standing with her arms outstretched. On each arm sat at least a dozen butterflies. More were on her head and one on her nose. We watched as some flew away and some arrived. Other people were watching this too.

We asked a docent if this was a Butterfly World act.

"No," he said. "This young girl comes often and the minute she arrives, the butterflies flock to her." He added that he had asked the parents if she wore flower perfume and their answer was no.

There seemed to be a love affair between this young girl and these butterflies. No one there knew why, so I suppose we will never know either.

We enjoyed our visit to Butterfly World and never forgot the young girl and her butterflies.

HAITI

Why we visited Haiti in the 1960s when Papa Doc (François Duvalier, dictator of Haiti from 1957 until his death in 1971) was still in power, I'll never know. Papa Doc was fighting his opponents in Cap Haitien, about 85 miles from where we were staying. I guess we visited Haiti because we were in the neighborhood–we had visited Jamaica and St. Croix on that trip, so from a geographical standpoint, Haiti made sense.

The abject poverty there was extreme and upsetting, but we found much that was beautiful as well. The island is a tropical paradise (it rained three hours every afternoon in July), and the local artwork of the Haitian people abounded. We bought good art including a carved wooden chest. When the chest arrived at Kennedy Airport, however, the FDA inspectors discovered it had termite bores. They allowed us to take it home, but only if we treated it with chlordane and kept it wrapped in plastic for three months, which we did.

We stayed in a wonderful resort in the mountains above Port-au-Prince. The food and service were excellent, but I know we were being watched by plain-clothed police.

One day, I found a huge water bug in the bathroom. (I'm not afraid of bugs and I knew that water bugs thrive in a tropical paradise.) I went to find the can of bug spray I had seen earlier on the staircase landing. The can was no longer there, so I reported the problem to the front desk. A female attendant arrived at our room immediately with a can of bug spray in her hand. Did she spray the bug? No.

First, she removed a large decorative hairpin from her head, stabbed the poor beast and then she sprayed it. We stood in shock as she performed this ritual which looked like voodoo. Or had experience taught her that bug spray was insufficient to defeat this enemy? In any event, that bug was double dead!

PESTS

BUGS IN MANHATTAN

We had just moved into our Manhattan apartment. I was sitting in our big for New York City eat-in kitchen at our glass-top table near a large window. Lo and behold, I looked down at the table and panicked when I saw a roach–at least I thought it was a roach. Then I realized, it was the reflection of a helicopter on the table.

MICE IN MIAMI

Mice always present problems in apartment buildings–they somehow get trapped in walls or move through radiators.

In my sister-in-law's condo in Florida, every afternoon at 3:00 pm, there would be scratching sounds on her kitchen wall. She thought she was hearing mice. I thought so too and so did the condo manager. The noise continued for more than a week before the manager decided to cut a hole in the wall.

I happened to be talking to my neighbor on the seventh floor who lived above my sister-in-law's apartment on the sixth floor. I never thought of asking her if she heard a noise in her kitchen wall. Coincidently, she told me that her children were always bored when they came home from school and that they skated in the kitchen. It took a few minutes for me to connect the dots. Why the noise of the ball bearings on the skates were heard in the wall, not on the ceiling, we will never know. But this time, it was not mice.

Luckily, the mystery was solved before demolition began.

SCHOOL STORIES

THE LOST TEST

I took a New York City Board of Education examination along with at least a dozen other art education students. We needed to pass this exam in order to teach art in New York City public high schools. Our teaching licenses would be awarded with our diplomas from Pratt Institute at graduation, and we would receive BFA (Bachelor of Fine Arts) degrees in painting and art education.

My adviser at Pratt Institute called me and said, "Your name is not on the grade sheet. Did you not take the test?"

"What, I sure did; there are many witnesses."

I called the Board of Education.

The secretary said, "Dear, you did not take the test or we'd have it." After I had screamed at her for five minutes, she said, "Come and find it."

I said, "Do what?"

She responded, "Come to my office and look for it."

And that's just what I did.

"You mean I can look in your file cabinets?"

"Yes."

I proceeded to look. Not very long into my search, on her desk under a huge pile of books and papers, lo and behold, there it was–my test.

She said, "Where did that come from?"

I said, "You're asking me?"

"I guess I took the test!"

DELETED

I returned to teaching after a four-year layoff. In 1975, the City of New York was broke and at the same time the Board of Regents of the State of New York changed the high school art requirement from two terms of minor art to one. Therefore, fewer art teachers were needed. This layoff didn't sit very well with me. I can easily imagine what it feels like for the breadwinner of a family to lose a job. My husband owned his own business, so we were not in financial jeopardy but it hurt. Being first on the city's layoff list, a job finally became available. I was reinstated in 1979.

When I returned to work, I was handed my profile, which we received every year that we were employed, indicating status and years of service. There were letter designations for status. "Status A" meant that you were in active service. Mine listed "Status D." The payroll secretary at my school called the Board of Education to inform them that I was not deceased. They told her, "The 'D' stood for deleted, not deceased."

SIZE MATTERS

All short people marvel when their children surpass them in height. One day that happened to me–except multiplied by a dozen.

The door of the large elevator in the high school where I taught opened. Inside was the basketball team. At least a dozen students, each six feet or taller, were squeezed into that space. They invited me in. All five feet one inch of me–I was intimidated. I refused. "I'll take the next one."

While I waited for the elevator to come again, I reflected, "Weren't they all at least one foot shorter last year?"

Photography by Joellen Bard

HONORS LEVEL HISTORY

Honors level history in high school was tough. I spent hours on the phone studying with a friend, so our homework was often similar. Perhaps it was too similar.

One day, the teacher collected homework and graded it. My friend and I were called to her desk. She asked, "Who copied from whom?" We explained how we studied on the phone. She didn't buy it!

Instead, she said, "You got a 90. Share it–you each got 45."

ACCIDENT

Driving in Brooklyn can be hazardous. I was involved in an accident at a busy Brooklyn intersection, 18th Avenue and 81st Street. I was traveling on 81st Street. A store located on the corner had double-parked their large truck right at the corner. Since I couldn't see the oncoming traffic on 18th Avenue, I slowly edged past the Stop sign. A speeding car on the other side of this two-way street caught my right front fender and dragged me across the intersection. The store, knowing that they were to blame for parking their truck illegally, immediately backed it into its garage.

When the police arrived, they blamed me one hundred percent for this accident because I went through a Stop sign. There was no other way to see, and I had honking cars behind me. Perhaps the police thought I should have flown.

They never asked if I were hurt; they just wanted my driver's license and registration. I had copies, not the originals. Since my pocketbook had recently been stolen, the police in my own neighborhood had told me to carry copies. These police disagreed. Luckily, my son was at home and he brought the originals. I think I would have ended up at the police station if I hadn't produced them.

The incident took place near the school where I taught. School had just ended for that day; therefore, many of my students witnessed this accident.

In the middle of the hullabaloo, a student in my guidance caseload tapped me on the shoulder, "Mrs. Bard, do you know my program for next term?"

Comic relief was definitely in order, but I had to be towed and I still got a ticket.

I ORDERED EIGHT CHAIRS AND GOT SEVEN TABLES

One morning, I opened the door–at least I tried to open the door–of my classroom. I was confronted with wall-to-wall furniture. I summonsed my boss who called the custodian to remove the furniture. Meanwhile, the students lined up in the hall. We all thought it was very funny, but couldn't understand why it happened.

Eventually, the mystery was solved: I had ordered eight new chairs to fit under large tables in my art room. It turned out that these chairs were no longer available from the New York City Board of Education supply list. They only listed the chairs which have attached arms. The secretary, in her infinite wisdom, did not consult with me or my boss, but ordered tables instead. When the eight tables came, my boss had no information about this fiasco, so he took one table for his office. Why the custodian crammed all those other tables into my classroom, I'll never know.

I ordered eight chairs and got seven tables. I never received the badly needed new chairs.

(The title *I Ordered Eight Chairs and Got Seven Tables* was the original title for my school story book begun 20 years ago. This project subsequently expanded into this book.)

CREATURE OF HABIT

For over ten years, the same teacher came into the teacher's lunchroom every day at the same time, ordered the same two hard-boiled eggs, took the same pepper shaker, and proceeded to the same seat.

He then mashed the eggs as he poured and poured the pepper. His plate turned olive green. I always thought that this would make a good art project. I didn't want to know how it tasted.

I too became a creature of habit. Every day for over ten years, I taught three classes in the morning, ate lunch at 11:30, and then proceeded to my guidance office for the rest of the day.

Even today, my stomach tells me that lunch is at 11:30 am.

BRAS

I taught painting for many years in adult education at Kingsborough Community College in Brooklyn, NY. I had wonderfully talented adult students who either worked in commercial art or who should have attended art school.

The funniest story is about a brassiere designer. "They make me go to Bloomingdales and Saks Fifth Avenue, buy the bras I like, cut them apart and reassemble them," he announced to the class. "I no longer like my job–I was trained to design, not to assemble."

The class roared with laughter and some elderly students turned red. "That is why I am here," he concluded.

PIERCING

A sophomore boy came to my guidance office. "Mrs. Bard, I need your help." He knew that I had a teenage son, so he asked, "Would you let your son pierce his ears?"

I thought for a few minutes before answering. "I wouldn't be happy about it, but at least the holes can close up; it's certainly better than alcohol or drugs."

The next day, I received a phone call from an irate, screaming mother. "How dare you give my son permission to pierce his ears."

It took a while to calm her down. Then I told her what had really happened. Fortunately, she responded with laughter. "If he'd only use his intelligence and creativity for school work, he could become a multi-millionaire," she said.

MY LAST CLASS TRIP

Over the years, I took many classes on trips from Brooklyn to Manhattan by subway, always with at least one chaperone, usually a parent. Why we were sent on long train rides instead of bus trips, I will never know. There were many trying experiences, including the fourth grader who fell asleep–I carried him off the train.

My most memorable trip was with a class of seniors majoring in art. These were bright and talented students, many of whom had applied to art colleges. They enjoyed the Museum of Modern Art and listened intently to the docent and asked intelligent questions. When it came time to discuss pieces they liked, one student chose a boxlike form sitting in the corner of the room–it was the humidifier. I don't remember how the docent handled that one, but I was laughing so hard, I left the room. I guess it looked like some of the other artworks.

The exasperating part of this story happened when we left the museum. Most of the students quickly dispersed and disappeared. These students were old enough to remain in Manhattan and not return to school with me, but they never had their parent consent forms signed. Instead, they just left the group. No way could I corral them. To boot, the train was delayed. There were no cell phones then and the telephones on the platforms were not working.

Finally, I returned to school with three students. The principal was impatiently pacing back and forth in front of the school building. He was furious.

"That's it," I said "That's my last class trip."

And it was!

SPECIAL STUDENT

One of my art education courses at Syracuse University required field experience. I volunteered at the local YMCA and worked one-on-one with special needs children. These five-year-old students had physical as well as mental disabilities. In retrospect, I guess I was doing art therapy.

I particularly remember one little girl. She was not achieving on level and was slated for a special kindergarten program. She was considered retarded, but the doctors weren't sure what her problem was.

I watched her closely as she colored and drew. When I demonstrated color mixing, she immediately copied what I had done. But when I gave her verbal instructions, she stared at me with a blank expression on her face. I told the parents that I thought she was deaf. They told me that her hearing had been tested. I pleaded, "Take her to an ear, nose and throat specialist at Upstate Medical Center at Syracuse University."

The parents listened and took her to a hearing specialist. They discovered that she had a 30 percent hearing loss in each ear. I suspect that because the child didn't hear well, she didn't listen.

The parents were so grateful. I still can't believe I was able to diagnose the problem when doctors couldn't.

WHAT A SURPRISE

Teachers rarely know what happens to the thousands of high school students they teach over the years. Once in a while, they may be lucky to catch a glimpse of the past.

I was working as a part-time college adviser in a private school after I retired from the New York City school system. One morning, I was standing in line at Dunkin' Donuts when a young lady tapped me on the shoulder.

"Mrs. Bard, do you remember me?"

I had no idea who she was.

"I am so and so… If you hadn't 'kicked my butt' and convinced me to attend art school, I wouldn't be where I am today. I am the art director of one of the largest New York advertising firms."

What a surprise! It rekindled my desire to know what had become of my other talented students, but I never did.

S'MORE SHORT SCHOOL STORIES

Teaching is a stressful job. The teacher's cafeteria was the place for relaxation and levity. We loved to share our stories:

We received records for two students, Ding Dong and Dong Ding. (We didn't know which was the first name and which was the surname since the inhabitants of many Asian nations give the surname first.) One student had a first grade reading level and the other a third grade reading level. Since the student/students never arrived, we never knew whether we were missing one or two students.

I was a part-time art teacher, part-time guidance counselor for many years. The students, for the most part, liked me because I helped so many of them–that's why they constantly followed me to the lady's room. I'd ask, "Can I please have five minutes of privacy?" And they'd still be standing right by the door when I came out.

My boss, the Assistant Principal of Art and Technology, came to observe my major art painting lesson. (Observations were required once per year by the New York City Board of Education.) I asked him if he would like to paint too, and he said yes. Because I was carrying too many supplies, and was anxious to start the lesson, I accidentally spilled water all over him. We were good friends and he laughed.

A student threw a pair of scissors from the back of the room to the front. Luckily, it didn't hit anyone. Asked why he threw the scissors, he said, "I was just passing it to my friend." The student was permanently removed from art class by the administration.

A student didn't feel well. She looked sallow. When I said that she looked green, an African-American student responded, "How can anyone look green?"

In another school where I taught, we had the largest percentage of Haitian students in New York City. The first snowstorm, they all simultaneously ran to the windows, opened them quickly and stuck their tongues out. I tried it too, but wasn't as excited as they were.

◎

Before knapsacks became the rage, boys used to fold a notebook and place the notebook and a pack of cigarettes in the front of their pants, behind the zipper. A biology teacher said she told the boys that she would not accept homework with crotch itch.

◎

Lay people do not understand the stress of teaching. People always say that teachers have vacations and summers off. Most teachers would not survive without those breaks. How many vocations mandate that you cannot use the bathroom? Teaching is one of them, since you cannot leave a class unattended. I could tell you some interesting experiences on that front.

◎

One student said to another student, "How did you get a 43 on that test? I got a 45 and copied the whole thing from you."

In hygiene class, the teachers used wooden models of penises to teach students how to put on and remove a condom. In our high school, these penises were made in the wood shop and each one was tied with a red bow. One day, some students brought all eight that they had made to show me. When they were lined up on my desk, they were a really funny sight. About two weeks after my private showing, a boy rushed into my classroom red-faced and as upset as one could be.

"They stole the penis," he shouted.

I was startled by what he said, and that class knew nothing of these wooden penises.

From the back of the room someone shouted, "Whose penis was stolen?"

There was such an uproar that teachers and administrators came running from their classrooms and offices. They thought that something terrible had happened.

This was the funniest incident in my long teaching career. As I write this story, I still laugh.

I worked in a special fourth through sixth grade reading/art program when I was laid off in 1976. These young students would not respond to their last names, so I lived a year with Daryl, Daryl, Darren, Derrick and Eric. Try that tongue twister.

I was listening to a lesson at the Brooklyn Museum. I don't remember what art project the teacher presented, but I do remember a question she asked these pre-schoolers.

"What foods do you keep in a freezer?"

A little boy answered, "Cheerios."

The teacher looked amazed and responded, "Why would you keep cereal in the freezer?"

The answer shocked me too—"So the roaches won't get into the box."

My friend decided to retire. "This was the last straw," she said. A student asked to borrow a pencil. The teacher asked him why he didn't bring one from home. The response, "I will not be a nerd."

A female student constantly chewed gum. When she was finished, she would put the wad inside the storage part of the desk. Despite my attempts to make her stop, she continued to chew gum, so my boss asked me to have her mother visit. When the mother walked in, she was chewing faster and louder than her daughter. What was I to say? I guess the apple really doesn't fall far from the tree.

When I began my guidance job, which included programming my caseload of students, I found a sign on the wall of my new office. It read: "You can pick your nose and you can pick your friends, but you can't pick your teachers." I left it there.

In one school where I taught, we had a student who could only read upside down. Why? The family owned one book, *The Bible*. Two sisters learned to read by sitting across from each other with the book between them. One read right side up; the other learned to read upside down.

I was so busy that I locked the door to my guidance office and hung a sign–"Gone Fishing." Many students asked the principal if I had really gone fishing.

Art students would invariably place their artwork against my face. I'd say, "If you move the paper away from my face, then I will see your work." Sometimes I would put the paper in front of their faces; then they got the point.

Twins, especially identical ones, loved playing games with people. They would invariably exchange classes and teachers didn't know who was who. Once, one identical twin was a talented artist, but the other wasn't. The untalented one knew she had to disappear before the drawing began. I used to kid her, "You are a good sneaking away artist." Once we had triplet boys. They created such havoc that we made sure all three had different classes.

It was my last term teaching. I had two "special" tables in my art room. At one table sat six Pakistani boys, each named Mohamed. At the next table were six Chinese girls, each with the surname Chang. I allowed students to choose their own seats, because I found that they were quieter when they sat with friends. I was so confused–unless they sat in their seats, I didn't know who was who. Invariably, one of these students would come to my desk for help and say, "Do you know who I am?" I was embarrassed to say that unless they were in their seats and I could look at the seating chart, the answer was, "No."

A Chinese boy who had just immigrated to the United States from China, without a word of English, was placed in the junior year based on his age. A year later, in his senior year, he took the SAT (Scholastic Aptitude Test) for college entrance. He received a 780 on the English portion of the test, an excellent score. When we asked him how he was able to score so high, he answered, "That was easy; I read the whole English dictionary." (This happened at a time when vocabulary was much more important on the SAT than it is now.)

NAME DROPPING

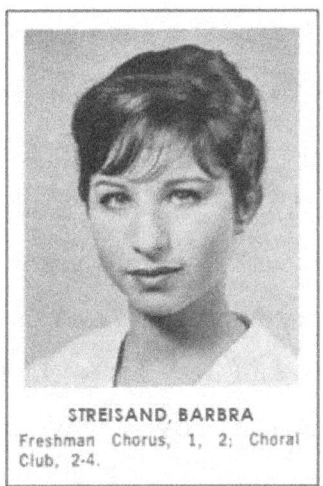

*The Arch, 1959, Yearbook of
Erasmus Hall High School, Brooklyn, NY*

BARBRA STREISAND

In 1959, I graduated from Erasmus Hall High School in Brooklyn, New York along with 1,500 other students–including Barbra Streisand. She was an acquaintance and perhaps she remembers me since she gave me permission to use the above photograph from our yearbook. I recall that she wore bobby socks and sneakers, but back then I didn't know that she sang. I guess that's why I was told I would pass music only if I didn't sing at graduation.

NAME DROPPING

During the Brooklyn Dodgers baseball seasons in the 1950s, Duke Snyder lived on my Brooklyn block. I used to rush home from school so that my friends and I could walk with him from the subway. I remember that he was very nice to us. When the Dodgers beat the Yankees in 1955, everybody celebrated in the streets. My parents told me that it looked like V-E Day (Victory in Europe Day) at the end of World War II.

When I was exhibiting in Soho, I frequently lunched at a restaurant on the corner of Prince and Wooster Streets. People were friendly and I often spoke to them. One day, I was reading an art magazine and there was a photo of Andy Warhol. I couldn't believe my eyes–he was one of the people I spoke to often. I realized then that I not only needed to read the art magazines, but I also needed to scrutinize the photos, so I'd know who was who.

Joe Paterno, of Penn State fame and infamy, visited me so I could vouch for one of my students who was about to receive a football scholarship. I gave the student a glowing report and he did play football for Penn State.

Gwen Verdon's son attended an art camp which I also attended. She watched my friend and me dance and commented favorably. What she didn't see was the huge black and blue mark on my hip, which was caused by falls that I didn't know how to do properly.

I recently ate lunch in a restaurant at the New York Botanical Gardens in the Bronx where I saw a wonderful Chihuly glass exhibit. Alan Alda was there with his wife and another couple. I was amazed–everybody stared at him, and I was pleasantly surprised that nobody bothered him.

I once saw Salvador Dali, with his handle-bar moustache and wearing his long black cape, on the arm of a tall blond model as he sauntered into an art gallery.

I was walking behind Jerry Orbach near City Hall in lower Manhattan when I realized that cameras were in front of him and that they were filming *Law and Order*. Since I watched every episode of that show, I assumed that I'd see myself on television. I did see the episode and recognized the scene, but I wasn't there. They had blacked me out.

I met Chuck Schumer, Senator from New York, several times in the early 70s in my neighbor's house. He was just beginning his political career and my neighbors used to run political parties for him. I've watched his long, successful career since then.

Gordie Howe is arguably the greatest hockey player of all times. He played 25 seasons for the Detroit Red Wings and 6 years for the World Hockey Association from 1946 to 1980. He was inducted into the Hockey Hall of Fame in 1972.

I met him in 1958. My high school friend was a hockey player and a hockey lover. He dragged me to Madison Square Garden all the time. I guess the night I met him, the New York Rangers were playing the Detroit Red Wings. We met him after the game. He knew my friend–I don't know how, but they spoke and Gordie Howe shook my hand.

There really is a Sara Lee. I bought Sara Lee baked goods for a very long time. But I have two personal connections to Sara Lee. The Sara Lee Corporation bought my friend's clothing manufacturing company, Host Apparel, Inc., about 17 years ago. And she rented our condo in Bal Harbour for a year when my husband and I were still working and couldn't spend the winter in Florida.

I met Carol Channing, singer, actress, dancer and comedian, known for the original *Hello Dolly*, when my college roommate, a theater major, interviewed her for the Syracuse University student newspaper. I don't know if she was performing for us, or if her unusual voice was just her. She spoke and acted like she did on stage.

WOODY ALLEN'S FAMILY

I knew Woody Allen's parents, Martin and Nettie Konigsberg and his younger sister, Letty Aronson, who has produced many of Woody Allen's films. The Konigsbergs owned a condo where my parents lived in Hallandale, Florida. My son and Woody Allen's niece and nephew, at a young age, used to play when I visited my parents and the Aronsons were in town too. My parents became very friendly with the Konigsbergs. In fact, they went to see *Hannah and Her Sisters* with them, and they were invited to one of Woody Allen's weddings. They did not attend and I don't know why.

Pleiades Gallery, Soho, 1978
Left to right bottom row–Nettie and Martin Konigsberg,
me, and my father
Photography by Arthur Bard

Coincidentally, the Konigsbergs lived near my Manhattan apartment, and I met and ate with them many times at a local diner. They came to one of my art exhibits in Soho and bought two paintings.

I also used to see Woody Allen and his wife, Soon-Yi Previn, walking on the Upper East Side. I watched the filming of his movie *Mighty Aphrodite* on 2nd Avenue. I lament that I never heard him play his clarinet which he does often at the Carlyle Hotel on East 76th Street.

NAMES

GREEN

My friend's friend Joan Green married Ron Green. She is now Joan Green-Green.

GEORGE

After the Tiananmen Square incident in Beijing, a terrified student came from China. His name was Fuque Hu. We immediately named him George and told him not to use his Chinese name. I don't remember whether we told him why, but I'm sure he quickly found out by himself.

THAI FOOD

My favorite dish in a local restaurant is PHUKET shrimp. Recently, I noticed that the name of the dish was changed on the menu to PUKET shrimp.

SMELLIE

"I got married–I'm not Smellie anymore. I'm now Jones, that is Lisa Jones."

I LOVE LUCY

My husband and I used to see Lucille Ball and Vivian Vance, who played Ethel Mertz, in the mid-60s, eating in our favorite Italian restaurant on Avenue M in Brooklyn. They were on Avenue M because NBC owned Studio I and II on Avenue M and East 14th Street.

NBC bought Vitagraph Studio from Time-Warner in 1951. There were two sound stages and a swimming pool in the complex which was used in *The Esther Williams Aqua Spectacular* in 1956. The film *Peter Pan* with Mary Martin was filmed there. NBC transformed this studio into the largest color TV studio when color TV became the rage. NBC sold the studio in 2000. It then became JC Studio where *As the World Turns* and *Another World* were taped with a live audience. JC Studio closed in 2015.

Research has revealed that many variety shows, including *The Kraft Music Hour, The Sammy Davis Jr. Show*, and *Sing Along With Mitch Miller* were taped there. Lucille Ball and Vivian Vance guest starred on one of those shows in the 1960s. *I Love Lucy* was filmed in Hollywood in the 1950s. (For more information about this historic Brooklyn site, log on to *EyesofaGeneration.com.)*

I LOVE SUSU

My cousin Sylvia–we called her Susu–was the daughter of my mother's oldest sister who had died in the Spanish flu epidemic in 1918. She had been raised by my grandmother along with my mother and her siblings. Years later when she was married, Susu and her husband lived on the same street as my parents in Brooklyn. And when I was a young child, she often took care of me.

Susu was a fabulous cook and often held family gatherings. Once, my mother and I were visiting while she was cooking a chicken in her pressure cooker. Suddenly, there was a tremendous POP. The pressure cooker had exploded and the chicken soared and stuck to her kitchen ceiling. Susu didn't know whether to scream or laugh. It turned out that we all had a good laugh. Then it came crashing down. What a mess!

I vividly remember the *I Love Lucy* episode in which the chicken stuck to the ceiling. Who would have ever thought that this would happen to cousin Susu? But it did!

PLANT NAMING

I have always named my cars. The last three were Whitey Ford (I'm an avid NY Yankees fan), Snazee and Grayboy.

My niece does that too, but she also names her plants: Ivy, Mary, and Sam. When I asked her why, she answered, "I feed them, I give them haircuts, I play music and talk to them so they should grow. Anything that I love and take such good care of needs a name."

AUNT SONIA

My mother was one of eight sisters, all born in Russia. The older sisters (I don't know how many) came to the United States around 1907. They worked in the garment industry until they had enough money to bring over their mother and younger sisters. I've looked at the Ellis Island manifest record, and found that they came to America in 1910.

All married except Aunt Sonia. She was the family "glue." She would visit everybody–sisters, nephews, nieces and friends and keep us all close. It was Aunt Sonia who made beautiful smocked dresses for all the little girls. I never forgot mine–it was light gray with red stitching.

She was an expert dressmaker. My mother told me that she worked at the Triangle Shirtwaist factory, but fortunately left before the famous fire. Later, Aunt Sonia's nine-to-five job was in the alteration department of a very prestigious dress shop. She fitted many celebrities including the Hollywood swim star, Esther Williams, and First Lady Mamie Eisenhower.

ROOSTER

While wheeling and dealing in the art world, I befriended some important art critics, including Dore Ashton and Lawrence Alloway. Lawrence Alloway was the critic who coined the term "Pop Art."

Lawrence Alloway once wrote an article for me about artist-run galleries. I included his article in the catalog of an art exhibit which I curated in Soho entitled *Tenth Street Days–The Co-ops of the 50s*. After a month in six Soho galleries, the exhibit then traveled to college art galleries and museums in New York State for two years.

I edited what Lawrence Alloway had written–at least, I thought I did. One night, I awoke suddenly and said to myself, "Oh, no. He wrote a 'rooster' of galleries and I meant to correct that to a 'roster' of galleries!" When I checked the page proofs of the catalog, it did indeed read "rooster." Can you imagine if I had left that error? Oh, would I have been embarrassed. It's hard to believe that I realized this in my sleep, especially since I rarely remember dreams. Thank goodness, I had found the error just in time. The page of the catalog was reset.

JOINT CHIEFS OF STAFF

On a hot summer's day, my friend and I lunched in an upscale west side restaurant before seeing a Broadway show.

At the restaurant, we were seated in a small empty room. Next thing we knew, there was a flood of activity as a large party of people were ushered in and seated. At one table was seated a man with five stars on the shoulder of his uniform who was sitting with civilians. At another table, there were six men, each dressed in military regalia.

The five-star general was Martin Dempsey, one of our previous Joint Chiefs of Staff under President Obama. We knew that he was in New York for a United Nations meeting and surmised he was lunching with family members, because there was a young boy seated at that table. The other six turned out to be his security team. When we left the restaurant, we saw three big black vans parked, and in front of each van stood a security guard with arms folded across his chest.

I guess they thought my friend and I were of little threat.

STORIES I'VE HEARD

KINDERGARTEN

My mother told me this story many times:

I couldn't wait to go to kindergarten. I probably should have gone to nursery school, but my parents didn't send me. I was reading before age four; I learned to read the advertisements on the subway going from Brooklyn to Washington Heights on the Upper West Side of Manhattan to visit aunts and cousins. We'd take the subway and then a double-decker bus up Fifth Avenue. No, this was not London. When I was a child, there were double-decker buses in Manhattan.

The first day of kindergarten, everyone cried. The teacher locked me in a big closet; I had no idea why. The dark brown wood closet in this very old school was at least eight feet by eight feet with coats hanging everywhere. I don't remember trying to get out of that closet, and I don't remember how or when I was released. But, I guess the closet incident really didn't faze me. I didn't tell my mother what happened, and I happily went off the school the following day.

My mother learned what had happened from other mothers; their children told them that I had been locked in the closet because I was crying. My furious mother went directly to the principal. I don't know what happened then, but I remember that we never saw that teacher again.

When my mother asked me why I was crying, I said, "I cried because everyone else was crying. I thought you were supposed to cry."

MARTHA'S VINEYARD

My friend and her family were vacationing in Martha's Vineyard. Her eight-year-old son was playing in the waves the whole day. He was exhausted when they finally made their way to a restaurant on a pier in a quiet residential neighborhood. Dinner was fine, but then...

The waitress was very slow to bring the check, so my friend gave her son the car keys. She told him to wait for them in the car, and to lock the door.

When the family finally arrived at the car, he was sound asleep, with the keys on the adjacent seat. It was 11:00 pm. There were no cell phones then, and no pay phones in sight. All the help in the restaurant had left; the restaurant was dark. Her husband and her two daughters knocked on the car windows, knocked with stones on the windows, and shook the car. He did not budge.

Her husband finally found a pay phone and called the police. The police came, but could not jimmy open the door. The police left. The family shook the car harder this time and the alarm went off. This didn't wake him either, but neighborhood people started to congregate.

Someone said, "What's wrong with that kid?"

My friend explained how tired her son was and that he was a very sound sleeper.

"No kidding," said the guy.

Someone else had an idea. He got a powerful boat light (a 50,000 candle power light) from his boat and shone that light in the boy's face.

That finally did it!

"Thank goodness," his mother thought. It was now 2:30 am.

He began to move and slowly opened his eyes. He looked around at all the people and, startled, he asked, "Am I in trouble?"

TWINS

This story I heard on Channel 4, NBC News, New York:

Approximately six sets of twins were born near midnight on New Year's Eve, 2016, in the United States–with this unusual twist. In each case, one twin was born just before midnight and the second twin was born just after midnight. This means that each twin has not just a different birth date, but also a different birth year.

There will be many two-day celebrations. If any school system uses January first as their cut-off date, these children could start school two different years.

"SNOPENING"

I heard this on YES, the NY Yankees Entertainment and Sports Network: Michael Kay, the Yankee's announcer proclaimed, "The Snopening Day at Yankee Stadium was canceled due to snow." The game was rescheduled for the next day, April 3, 2018.

WHO HAS MY MONEY

My friend told me she finally had a story for me:

She needed to pay her share of a collection for a condo barbeque. She put the cash in an envelope and wrote the neighbor's name on the front. Then she left the envelope on the kitchen counter, so she could remember to give it to her neighbor later.

My friend's husband never posts the mail, but for some reason, this time he put the letter in the mailbox. Apparently, he didn't notice that it needed both an address and a stamp. Of course, it also had no return address

My friend called the post office.

They said, "Forget it, the letter is already in the distribution center in Newark."

My friend laughed as she told me this. She asked, "Who has my money?"

GOOD LAUGHS

FACING THE SEA

My mother told me this story:

A long time ago on the French Riviera, my father used to stand in the water looking at the beach, so he could see the nude women as they changed back into their clothing. He contended that the women faced the Mediterranean, so they couldn't be seen nude by people sitting on the beach. My mother had a good laugh thinking about games people play.

FLUSH

My friend's husband got up from the toilet in the bathroom at work. He does not know how, but the expensive glasses that he was wearing fell into the toilet. He stood and watched as the automatic flushing toilet ate his glasses.

EXCHANGE STUDENT

My friend told me this story:

Her daughter had been an exchange student in France. When it came time for the French student to come to America, the French girl's mother called my friend. She asked, "Should my daughter bring a one-piece or a two-piece bathing suit?"

My friend answered, "Either."

The girl arrived with her one-piece suit–a bottom.

They went shopping for a bathing suit.

SWINGING

My friend knows that I love horses. When she heard that I had included several horse stories in this book, she wanted her story to be included:

In camp in the Catskills, she learned to horseback ride. She loved it and rode every day. Once they were on a wooded path. She misjudged the height of the branches and suddenly she was hanging from a tree like one would see in a slapstick movie. The horse followed the pack, no rider on his back. She was hanging too high to jump, swinging back and forth. She was half screaming, half laughing as the group leader brought the horse back and helped her jump from tree to horse. She was scared at the time, but that never deterred her from riding again.

INTO THE LAKE

My husband was a good horseback rider. He loved horses and he loved to ride. In fact, he sometimes led groups for a stable in Brooklyn's Prospect Park.

This is a story he laughed about time and again:

One hot summer day, he went riding along the horse path in Prospect Park. Suddenly, his horse made a detour that took them to Prospect Park Lake. Then she took him for an involuntary swim. He imagined what it would have been like if he had been guiding a group of riders.

How embarrassed he was when he returned to the stable. The owner couldn't believe what had happened, because that mare was usually very obedient and my husband knew how to handle horses. He guessed that she was so hot that nothing would deter her from entering the water.

My poor husband went home soaking wet.

HORSE TICKET

My cousin has always been a horse lover. As a young teen, he worked a variety of jobs to earn spending money. And the best way, he thought, to spend the money he earned was to take the subway to Van Cortlandt Park in the Bronx to horseback ride. The park had stables and miles of bridle paths.

One day, the horse he was riding was bitten by a bug. The animal reared up, galloped onto the pedestrian pathway, and fell to the ground. Fortunately, my cousin reacted quickly, jumped off the horse and was not hurt.

Then, to make matters worse, he was approached by a policeman who issued my cousin a ticket for riding off the bridle path. No amount of explanation about bugs and bites could sway the cop's mind.

Feeling totally justified in his defense, my cousin showed up in court to explain exactly what had happened. Unfortunately, the judge, just like the policeman, didn't want to hear any excuses.

"If I hear one more word from you, I'll double the fine," he said.

No justice here. Sad to say, that put an end to my cousin's horseback riding in Van Cortlandt Park.

Photography by Millicent McKinley

DEAD HORSE

A fellow bridge player and friend told me this story:

When my friend and her sister were teenagers, they were allowed to bet on a horse race while they were vacationing with their parents in Montreal. They had no idea how to choose a winner, but they guessed and placed a two-dollar bet on a horse called Steinway High. They were very excited at the prospect of winning.

The horses rounded the track once. On the second round, Steinway High sat down. Her sister was not paying attention and my friend tapped her on the shoulder and said, "Our horse is sitting." Then the horse lay down, dead.

The race was stopped. People were crying and running on to the track to find out what had happened. The sisters looked at each other and even though they were upset, they tried not to laugh. They had bet on a dead horse.

Neither of them ever bet on a horse again.

MY FATHER'S TALES

My father loved to tell stories. He was the consummate storyteller:

IT PAYS TO LISTEN

My father enjoyed horse racing. There was a racetrack, Gulfstream Park, near where my parents lived in Hallandale, Florida.

One day, my father was at the track. He was selecting a horse on which to bet when he overheard this conversation. "Make sure you bet on #8. He will surely win." So, he bet on that horse. The horse did win and my father proudly pocketed $800. From the conversation he had heard, he surmised that the race was fixed.

When he arrived home, my mother was surprised with the win, but when she heard that the race was probably fixed, she was ready to return the money.

SPRING TRAINING

My father attended spring training games when the NY Yankees Spring Training Camp was in Fort Lauderdale. There were many roped-off parking lots with numbers near that field. You were required to pre-pay parking, so he paid, parked, and made sure to remember the number of the lot. When the game ended, he proceeded to his lot. The number was missing and so were the ropes. It was a sea of cars and roaming people.

My father and many others were lost. He found his car two hours later.

THE BEST EXCUSE

I heard this identical story from a teacher friend and from my father who also taught:

A student was absent for a test. When he returned the next day, he apologized to the teacher.

"I missed the test because my grandmother died," he explained.

A week later, once again he missed a test. This time he said, "My grandmother is very ill."

The teacher said, "I thought you told me last week that your grandmother passed away."

He responded, "I guess she got a little better."

HOME SWEET HOME

My long-time friend owns a house in Brooklyn and rents an apartment in Manhattan. Since the death of her husband over a year ago, she has been preparing the house for sale, planning to move permanently to Manhattan.

There had been pipe and water problems in the house for a long time, so my friend and her husband, who were travelers, had special water sensors installed. If a problem arose, the water would shut off automatically. Everything was fine for years.

Since her mini-move and her attempt to ready the house for sale, she has had nothing but water problems again. Six months ago, a pipe burst and she worked with her insurance company and their contractors–a beautiful new floor was installed in the den. The real estate agent was finally ready to put this house on the market.

Returning from Manhattan two months ago, she opened the front door and screamed. Mega-damage again–walls down, ceilings hanging, floors up. With this second flood, the water sensor malfunctioned.

What to do? I suggested that she sell the house, "as is." But she didn't. She was determined to fetch the best price, and she renovated again.

At that point, she believed that her house didn't want to be sold. I agreed with her. Strange things were happening here!

There is a final chapter to this story: renovation was completed. The real estate agent ran an open house and 80 people showed up. It is a nice house; however, neither she nor the agent can figure out why so many people came. There was a bidding war and the house was immediately sold for more than she had asked.

THE COFFEE MAKER

This story was told to my friend. She laughingly told it to me:

When her friend's husband and her friend gave dinner parties, the wife always served espresso at the end of the meal. She used a traditional Italian espresso pot which had two halves. The water went in the bottom half. When the water boiled, the procedure was to grasp the two handles firmly and turn it upside down. This procedure was never a problem for her.

But when her sister-in-law saw her turning the pot upside down, she was shocked. She said, "You could get burned with that thing! There's a new, more modern espresso maker. The coffee is just a good and you don't have to turn it upside down."

Deferring to her older, more knowledgeable sister-in-law, she bought the newfangled coffee maker. She read the instructions carefully, and the next time they had a dinner party, she used it.

After their guests left, her husband said, "Something was wrong with the coffee tonight. It didn't taste very good." And she said, "I don't know why. I read the instructions for the new coffee maker carefully."

It wasn't until she dismantled the coffee maker to wash it that she discovered what was wrong. She had brewed the instructions along with the coffee.

SUV ON FIRE

My dentist told me this story:

A year ago, my dentist and his wife attended a charity luncheon at a local country club. They enjoyed themselves and even won two raffles, dinner at a restaurant in town and a basket of many bottles of wine.

When the affair ended, they drove to his dental office to collect important papers that he needed. As they were driving, they thought they smelled something burning. After opening the car window, they decided that the smell had come from barbeques at a street fair in town.

When they got to his office, he went inside; his wife remained in the car. A few minutes later, his wife frantically ran after him–the smell was indeed coming from their one-year-old SUV. He quickly ran to the car to retrieve other important papers; his wife grabbed the wine and called 911.

They stood and watched as the hood of the car became engulfed in flames. The police and the fire department came quickly and the firemen extinguished the fire. My dentist and his wife gasped when they saw the scant remains of their car. It was totaled.

When they finally arrived home, shaken but safe, they drank to their luck with the wine they had won that day.

Photography by Dr. Jack Elbaum

They were thankful that they were not hurt and grateful for the quick service from the fire and police departments. However, they have been unable to stop thinking about worse scenarios: they could have been stuck in the car, or the car could have been parked in their garage and their house could have caught fire.

The insurance company did an "autopsy" on the car, but was unable to determine the cause of the fire. My dentist and his wife received the insurance money and bought a new car.

One of the fireman remarked as he was leaving, "This will be a great story to tell friends and family for years to come."

He was right. This happened one year ago, and they are still telling their story!

MY ISRAELI FRIEND

My friend is a Sabra, a term that denotes someone who was born in Israel. She is one of a number of friends who were born outside the United States, who lived through the immigrant experience, and who became U.S. citizens as soon as they could. Other close friends hail from Jamaica, Iran, Peru, France, Germany, Hungary, and Canada. Some came to the United States as refugees.

My friend's mother went to Palestine from Germany and her father went from Czechoslovakia, both in the mid-1930s.

Her father was so anxious to immigrate to what he rightly thought would become Israel that he jumped from a ship that was blockaded by the British and swam to shore. Her parents met and were married in Palestine. My friend was born and ten years later, in 1953, they immigrated to America.

The family left Israel because they wanted to be with my friend's maternal grandfather who had been living in the United States since 1940 or 1941. Miraculously, U.S. relatives had been able to extricate him from a Nazi camp in southern France in 1940 or 1941. My friend's mother hadn't seen her own father since World War II.

German was my friend's first language; Hebrew was her second language. She spoke no English, but was put into fifth grade because she had finished the fourth grade in Israel. She learned English quickly, but not without some struggle; for example, in the sixth grade, she kept a notebook with photographs under which she was required to put captions. Under a scene of a beach she wrote, "Scene of a Bitch."

When I interviewed my friend for this story, I asked her if she remembers her early childhood experiences in Israel, including the Israeli War of Independence in 1948. She said, "yes." She vividly remembers having to quickly leave Jerusalem as the War of Independence intensified.

She was raised like a European–she holds utensils the European way, fork in left hand, knife in right hand. When she learned English, she replaced Hebrew and subsequently forgot it. She continued to speak German at home.

My friend's birth certificate reads, "Born in Palestine." She was born before Israel became a state. She holds dual citizenship and two passports. When she visits Israel, she enters with her Israeli passport; when she returns to the United States, she enters with her American passport.

You would think she had been born in America. She has no accent. She attended college, held a good job, raised a family and now has grandchildren.

Immigrants bring vitality and diversity to our nation. That's what makes the United States special. I hope we continue that legacy!

MY NEIGHBOR'S TALES

My neighbor and friend "got it." When I explained my project, she immediately typed these four stories. She laughed when she handed them to me. She said, "I can tell you many more." These are her stories:

PRESIDENT

My neighbor's husband was the president of a small pharmaceutical company. My neighbor accompanied him on a business trip to Paris where they met a business associate at a fancy restaurant.

The French associate and a well-dressed, elegant woman were seated at a table waiting for them. When my neighbor was seated, she started a conversation with the woman. They talked as the men discussed business. In the course of their conversation, my neighbor learned that the woman didn't have any children.

It wasn't until later that she learned: this was his mistress, not his wife.

MISTAKEN IDENTITY

The same neighbor and her husband attended a very important political dinner at the Waldorf Astoria Hotel in New York City. With thousands of attendees, they were seated at "the table" with Newt Gingrich and the CEOs of Walmart, CVS, and Duane Reade. They had no idea why they were seated there with all those important people.

Chuck Schumer was the keynote speaker. When he finished speaking, he came to the table and shook her husband's hand. This act in this kind of setting usually denotes ultimate VIP status. Again, they were baffled.

It turned out, her husband and her husband's brother could have passed for identical twins. The brother was seated far away in this crowd. They eventually realized that this was a case of mistaken identity. The brother was a big Chuck Schumer supporter. Who knew that the wrong couple was seated at "the table?"

THE BUNGALOW

Every summer in the 1950s, my neighbor's parents would rent a bungalow in the Catskills. My neighbor, her mother, and her three brothers would spend the summer there. Her father would drive up on weekends.

One summer, the owners of this bungalow colony had a new building added. Her mother immediately moved them into this new facility. When her father arrived late Friday night, he opened the door of the original bungalow and scared the pants off the new occupants.

My neighbor's mother had simply forgotten to tell her father that they'd moved.

THE POEM

When my neighbor was in second grade, she wrote a poem and was very proud of it. It went something like this:

"A picture to me is like the sun in the sky,

Like the birds way up high,

Like the trees, the flowers, the busy buzzing bees,

A picture can mean many things,

But, it brings to me the birds that sing,

A picture can mean anything."

The teacher called my neighbor to her desk and said that she could not have possibly written that poem. She was devastated and never wrote another poem!

SILVER

Victimized and terrorized by World War II, my future mother-in-law, her three daughters, and her nine-year-old son, left Turkestan, Kazakhstan when the war ended in 1945. They had spent four dire years in Turkestan after arriving from northwestern Russia in 1941. They were heading back to Poland from where they had been exiled by the Nazis in 1939. From there, they eventually arrived at a DP camp in Germany. (See page 68, "Starving Children.") They had never been in a concentration camp, but they suffered terribly during those years. They were survivors!

One of my sisters-in-law recently told me that they had heard a train was leaving Turkestan, heading for Moscow. They quickly readied themselves and a man helped them to the railroad station with their scant belongings. The man pushed the family into the overcrowded cattle car. There were no seats, so they sat in a corner on the floor. At the same time that all these people were leaving, a goodly number were arriving. They were Russian soldiers dressed in uniform returning from the front. Each soldier carried a duffle bag.

Her mother found a bag on the floor that was left behind. It was brimming with silver–candlesticks, urns and a menorah. They determined that the goods were worth a fortune and that they could sell the items in Moscow. Then they feared that they might be arrested for looting.

What does one do to rid oneself of all this silver? Every time the train stopped, they threw out one piece.

My sister-in-law laments that they didn't keep the menorah.

CANDELSTICKS

My friend's mother, one of six siblings, was born in the United States in 1905, but her oldest brother was born in Poland before the family immigrated. At age 16, after the family came to America, this brother went swimming and caught a cold which turned into pneumonia.

This was a time before antibiotics, and he did not survive the pneumonia. After the death of his son, my friend's grandfather, in his grief and anger, threw a beautiful silver candlestick across the room. It hit something and the candlestick was bent.

My friend doesn't know what the candlestick hit, but this beautiful pair of candlesticks, brought from Poland, still bears the mark of anger.

These candlesticks are used every Jewish holiday and this story is told and retold.

THE HOUSE IN POLAND

My brother-in-law told me this story:

After eight terrible years of war and its aftermath, my future mother-in-law and future husband arrived in the United States in 1947. As excited as they were when they saw the Statue of Liberty in New York Harbor, that's how disappointed they were when they saw the west side of Manhattan.

They were driven to their new home in Brooklyn by the American relatives who had pleaded for the Bard family to come to the U.S. before World War II. My future father-in-law had resisted the move then. He was a successful businessman and in their small bucolic town, few realized what would transpire.

My future brother-in-law had immigrated to the U.S. in 1938. He had worked, and then fought in the American Army in the Pacific during World War II. He had purchased the house in Boro Park, Brooklyn when he learned that his family was finally coming to America.

They arrived in Boro Park. My future mother-in-law got out of the car, looked across the street at a typical two-family Brooklyn brick house and proclaimed, "My house in Poland was much prettier."

Where the house in Brok, Poland was, now stands the town's municipal building and post office.

The Bard house in Brok, Poland
(Top window): Martin Bard and friend
(Right bottom): Dora, Simcha Dovid, Hilda, and Yankel Bard

AGELESS / TIMELESS

THE SILLY QUESTION
Teachers ask thousands of questions. Sometimes a question misses the mark. My 35-year-old English teacher friend told me this story:

Her English class was reading Macbeth. She asked a silly question, "Was Lady Macbeth older or younger than me?" The answer, "Oh no, you're much older than Lady Macbeth."

IS IT DAY OR NIGHT?
This story was told by a friend:

As a child, my friend had the good fortune of having a dad who worked for an airline, so her family spent time traveling. On one trip, they arrived in London in the morning and forgot to reset their watches appropriately. They were so tired that they took a nap. When they woke, they didn't know how much time had passed. Their watches said five o'clock, but they had no idea whether that was day or night.

Her mother, always the practical one, said, "Let's go to a restaurant and see if they give us a breakfast menu or a dinner menu."

This was a fun game. They went to a restaurant near their hotel and they gave them the dinner menu. That was how they found out it was evening.

OLD

My friend told me that her mother was a "character." She went into a nursing facility at about age 80.

My friend asked her mother, "Why don't you go downstairs? There are so many nice things to do there: concerts, games, art."

Her mother responded, "I'm not going down there. The people are too old."

Then my friend asked her mother, "Why don't you get a hearing aid?" Her mother answered, "Why bother, all my friends are deaf."

IS IT NIGHT OR DAY?

After our weekly Tuesday evening bridge game, my upstairs neighbor said that she had had a weird experience the night before. This is her story:

After a busy day, she ate dinner, undressed early, and sat down on the couch to relax. This was at 7:00 pm. She fell asleep and woke at 9:45 pm. "Oh my God," she murmured to herself, "I have an appointment at 10:00." She quickly got up and got dressed. Ready to leave, she looked out the window. It was dark.

Her appointment was for 10:00 am the following day.

UNKNOWN CIRCUMSTANCES

ANGRY

My friend's daughter, age three, said, "I'm so angry that I'm going to tell God on you." She walked outside, looked up and said, "God…" and then stopped. The problem: neither she nor her mother could remember why she was so angry.

PICKETING

Another friend, who was a teacher, spent much time in the late 60s and the early 70s picketing. The teachers in New York City staged many strikes against the Board of Education in the days before New York State passed the Taylor Law, which took two days of pay away for every day picketing.

One day, her nine-year-old son made a picket sign that said, "Mommy and Daddy Unfair to Frank." He walked around the living room with his picket sign for three hours. The problem was the same: none of them could remember why he was picketing.

SHORT QUIPS

My friend's three-year-old daughter said, "Mommy, mommy, come look, the crocuses fainted."

My husband pulled a light chain–New York City went black. His business partner accused him of causing the blackout.

During a downpour, a stranger turned to my friend and said, "Take off those beautiful yellow suede shoes and put them in your pocketbook before you ruin them."

When my neighbor's uncle retired, he became so "pesty" that her aunt said, "If Blue-Cross, Blue-Shield would pay for it, I'd get a divorce."

TOTEM POLES

The Tlingit Indians have lived in southeast Alaska for at least 11,000 years. Today they number about 17,000 people. They follow many ancestral practices, including totem pole carving. These poles record legends and histories of the many Tlingit clans.

When I was on my Alaskan cruise, I saw many totem poles in Saxman Village, a Tlingit village in Ketchikan, Alaska. They are impressive! At a lecture in Saxman Village, I learned that anthropologists are not sure whether the Tlingits came from Polynesia or across the Aleutian landmass. They also cannot date many of the old totems, but they are now being preserved. The Indian Division of the Civilian Conservation Corps has restored old poles and has copied damaged ones.

Photography by Millicent McKinley

During the cruise, I met a retired geologist who had worked on numerous land-clearing projects in Alaska. He told me this story:

His team was set to clear trees from a large tract of land. One engineer looked and remarked, "These are very strange looking trees."

He was right; they were not trees. They were moss-covered totem poles. This turned out to be an abandoned Indian village, probably Tlingit or Haida Indian. Many such abandoned villages have been found in southeast Alaska. The Alaskan Indian tribes were decimated by disease as were the American Indian tribes, and this is the probable cause of the abandoned villages.

EASTER AT ALICE

My editor tells her story:

In 1967, when she was six years old, her parents took their three kids for a vacation in the Australian Outback. When Americans think of the Outback, they usually think of a dry desert. This is true, but sometimes there can be flash floods that last for days. This happened when the family was in Alice Springs. All the roads were under water, and so was the landing strip for the small planes that were used for transportation.

Not much is grown locally in the Outback. For the most part, the residents are cattle ranchers, and apparently some people kept chickens for local use. There was plenty of food in town, so nobody was going to starve, but unfortunately there was little variety. My editor remembers having steak and eggs for breakfast, steak and eggs for lunch and steak and eggs for dinner.

What really upset the Australians, however, was that they had run out of beer. Easter was coming, and there was no beer! How could they celebrate Easter properly? They managed to arrange for a plane to drop an emergency load–all of it beer.

Luckily, my editor's mother had brought Easter chocolate with her when they flew to Alice Springs. The Easter Bunny came for the kids at least, and the residents of Alice Springs had their beer for Easter.

BRIDGE

This story was told by a fellow bridge player:

Bridge is a difficult and addictive game. She is addicted and so am I. They claim that bridge keeps you "sharp." I hope that's true.

Recently, she received a very good hand. She wondered how often she could expect to get such a hand. In fact, I wondered–how many bridge combinations exist.

Once, our long-term bridge teacher received a hand with 13 spades. Mathematicians calculate odds: our teacher is a mathematician, so I asked him to calculate the odds of such a hand. We learned that there are 615,013,559,600 possible combinations. Yes, you read that correctly, over six-hundred billion combinations. Since only one of those combinations has 13 spades, the odds are only one hand in 615,013,559,600. Hard to believe, but true (Robin Gillett, certified bridge teacher).

For bridge players: he knew that 13 spades meant a grand slam, but he did not bid 7S directly. Instead, he risked starting with a Pass! He later entered the auction, eventually bidding 7S which was doubled by his opponents, just as he hoped it would be. He redoubled, claimed all 13 tricks, and received a mega-score (vulnerable–2940 points). That's risky, but good, creative bridge playing.

TREASURE

My friend heard this story. We have permission to tell it, but the storyteller wants to remain anonymous:

This storyteller's favorite hobby is to rummage at garage and estate sales. He is particularly fond of buying used watches. At one such sale, he bought a Naval watch since he had served in the Navy. He paid $25.

While he was searching for watches on the internet, he discovered that only 100 Naval watches like the one he had bought were produced. Further research revealed that it was worth a significant amount of money.

He and his wife took the watch to Sotheby's auction house in NYC for an appraisal. They were told it was worth over $100,000, and he was invited to sell the watch at auction. His watch was featured in the auction catalog. The first bid was $60,000, and it sold for $140,000

I often watch *Antiques Roadshow* on TV, and I see situations like this all the time. I've also taken antique watercolor paintings to Sotheby's for appraisal, but they were not worth what I thought they should be. But I never before knew anyone who actually had found such a treasure!

BETS

BLACKJACK

I heard this story "through the grapevine," and it is just too good not to be told:

Someone played blackjack in Atlantic City and won $20,000. He collected the money and immediately went to a jewelry store where he purchased a $20,000 Rolex. Oh, did he love that watch.

Then his wife and he went on vacation. He hid the watch somewhere in his house, so it would be safe while they were away. It was never found!

JACKPOT

My father and his friend won $10,000,000 in the Florida lottery, they thought. What excitement! What to do? He called his lawyer who told him that the first step was to report his winning to the store where he had bought the ticket.

They quickly ran to the store. To their amazement and despair, they hadn't won after all. This is hard to believe–they had looked at the wrong stub. They thought they had won on a Wednesday. They had looked at the Tuesday ticket which had the exact numbers that won on Wednesday. What are the odds of that? What a disappointing coincidence.

They hadn't won any money, but they had won a lot of laughs.

PARIS METRO

This story was told by an anonymous storyteller:

This storyteller and his girlfriend were in the Paris Metro in 1992. Since he did not heed the warnings about suitcases and turnstiles, the inevitable happened.

Turnstiles in Paris and in some other European cities are different from the ones in the U.S. They are not really turnstiles, since they have two plexiglass sliding doors which open outward, but people still call them that. You insert a cardboard ticket into a ticket slot and then retrieve your ticket on the other side of the turnstile, once you have passed through. You can see pictures of these turnstiles on the internet.

The storyteller's girlfriend had already passed through her turnstile. He was wearing a large steel-framed backpack on his back. He inserted the ticket into the slot, and the plexiglass doors opened, and he proceeded through, but the backpack didn't. The sliding doors had closed in between his back and the backpack, which was now stuck on the other side. He could not pull it through the small gap and could not go back through the doors either. He also could not get his arms out of the straps. What to do?

He decided to try to slide the backpack upward in the "slot" that had been created by putting one leg on the turnstile structure on each side and pushing up. He had hoped to climb high enough so that the backpack would slide up over the top of the doors, but that didn't happen. Instead, the top of the backpack frame hit the low ceiling above the doors, and he could not free himself. He had no choice but to jump back down off the turnstile, but unfortunately that too became impossible. He found himself dangling two feet off the ground. By now, everyone there was laughing, but no one knew what to do.

Thank goodness, some other bystanders were able to come to the rescue and pull the two doors all the way apart, freeing the backpack.

He is still laughing when he tells his story, but it was such a silly, unbelievable situation, he doesn't want anyone to know who he is.

SPECIAL SERVICE DOG

My neighbor's daughter owns a beautiful golden retriever, Labrador mix. I see this young lady walking the dog all the time, but I only recently heard this story:

The beautiful 24-year-old daughter has epilepsy, a neurological disorder that causes seizures. At age eight, she had a seizure that resulted in brain damage. The mother, who resides with her, is a nurse. She has sought to find the best medical treatment and support to help her daughter feel independent and safe.

Through the FACES Parent's Network at New York University Langone Hospital, they discovered a non-profit organization, Canine Assistants, which trains dogs specifically for certain medical purposes. These dogs only assist people with diabetes, MS and epilepsy. I have seen service dogs trained to sniff for drugs and bombs in airports and therapy dogs making sick people smile in hospitals, but I had very little knowledge about what breeds are used for what purposes and no knowledge about the differences in dog training programs.

"It's like waiting for an organ for transplant," said my neighbor's daughter. It took over seven years on a list. In February 2016, this young lady was selected as a recipient of a Canine Assistants seizure response dog. (Dogs like this cannot be bought.)

Photography by David Scott

This is a very special dog. There is a strong "bond" between the dog and the owner/patient. "He is the most affectionate companion and cuddly friend. He makes me feel safe when I am alone," she said. They were trained together at a two-week camp in Georgia. The dog is with her all the time, day and night. He monitors her condition and if he senses a seizure, he immediately brings her medicine. He has even awakened her at night when he has sensed a problem. He has a special "dog telephone." When told to push, he pushes a button with his paw and contacts the mother. This has worked more effectively than dialing 911.

They recently found a job for her and her companion. She is working in an orthodontist's office and the dog is working too. He has found a place consoling crying children in the office.

As wonderful as this situation is, owning a dog like this sometimes creates problems. They often fly to Florida to visit the young woman's grandmother. How this large dog can fit under the seat and remain still for over a two-hour flight is mind-boggling to me, but he does it. He has been trained not to bark and I've never heard him bark. People get angry that a disabled person can bring a large dog on the plane and they can't. And passengers try to abuse the "service system" on airplanes, trying to bring on service monkeys and service turkeys, I was told. He wears a vest that reads "Do Not Pet," but it is difficult for people to stay away from this cute and affectionate dog.

It's a pleasure to know these people and to watch this beautiful dog constantly at work.

THE THANKS THAT KEEPS ON GOING

My physical therapist told me this story:

Finishing his master's degree in physical therapy at Northeastern University in Boston, he was required to complete a clinical internship at Children's Hospital in Houston.

His first patient was a four-year-old boy with cystic fibrosis, named Tyler. Within two weeks, they developed a strong bond.

One day, the therapist arrived at the hospital. He walked into the room and found it bare. There were no balloons, no flowers, no family pictures. The bed had been made up with fresh sheets. He learned that the child had passed away during the night.

Later, he saw the family and began to cry because this was his first patient death. The family consoled him when it should have been the reverse. The parents said, "Thank you for making Tyler's last days so pleasurable."

Twenty-four years later, he still receives a Christmas card from this family with the names of the parents, the two children subsequently born, and Tyler.

OBEDIENT ANIMALS

DOG

Every year, when my teacher friend returned to work at the end of the summer, her dog would make a statement. It was as if the dog thought "I'll get even with you." And she did–every year!

My friend and her husband had created a rock garden on the side of their living room–small pebbles and potted plants.

Each September, on the first day that my friend was away at school, the dog would move a pile of pebbles to the middle of the living room floor. When my friend returned home and found the pebbles, she would reprimand the animal and return the pebbles to the rock garden. On Day Two, there would be a smaller pile of pebbles and Reprimand Number Two. On Day Three, an even smaller pile and Reprimand Number Three. On the fourth day, there would be just one pebble in the middle of the floor. And there would continue to be one pebble on the floor every day for a week. Then the game would end until the next year.

She and her dog understood each other very well.

CAT

A former student told me this story:

Her eight-week-old kitten was always very affectionate, but he always wanted attention. She soon discovered that she could not read the morning newspaper without disruption from him.

As she picked up the newspaper, he would charge into the paper with all his kitty-might and energy; then he'd run away in a flash. This occurred every morning for a week and as hard as she tried, she was unable to grab and reprimand him.

One morning, she pretended to be reading, but was fully on guard to nab the perpetrator. As soon as he made his move, she picked him up by the scruff of the neck as a mother cat would do and scolded, "You bad boy, out!"

She threw him into the hallway and slammed the door shut. After relaxing with her paper and a cup of coffee, she opened the door and let him in. With his head and tail hung low and dejected, that cat looked remorseful. He never charged her paper again.

They had a mutual love and understanding.

ALONE AND COLD

I have a friend who grew up in Montreal, Canada. She has never forgotten this story from her young childhood:

In Montreal in winter, it's dark by 4:00 pm. She was bored and wanted to go outside. Her mother told her that it was too cold and too dark just to take a walk or play outside. Also, since there was no snow just then, it wouldn't be any fun to play outside.

My friend insisted and made her mother so miserable that she finally dressed the little girl in her winter clothes. That was no easy task–ski pants, sweater, jacket, boots, etc.–and it took her mother a good ten minutes. When she finally finished, her mother opened the door and said, "Go outside." Her mother watched attentively from the window. She was set to teach my friend a lesson–it is no fun to go outside alone with nothing to do.

Of course, her mother knew that after a few minutes, my friend would be ready to go inside, but she let her stay out a little longer to reinforce "the lesson."

Then a stranger came by. The woman rang their doorbell. My friend's mother opened the door and was greeted angrily. "Why are you leaving your young child outside alone in the dark and cold?"

Her mother let the little girl come into the house. When I asked my friend if she learned "the lesson," she answered, "No, and knowing my personality, I probably never did."

WOOF, WOOF

I think it must have been pre-stroller days, so I must have been very young. My father told me this story:

He loved to walk with me in my carriage around our six-story apartment house neighborhood in the Flatbush section of Brooklyn.

I would look up, point and say "woof, woof." No birds were in sight.

My father would think, "What could she be seeing?"

One day, as my father was looking up trying to solve the mystery, I fell out of the carriage. Then, he inadvertently ran me over with it. He did, however, solve the mystery that day. He realized that I was seeing gargoyles on the façade of some buildings.

I guess I survived the fall, since I am still here to tell these tales.

AUTHOR'S AFTERTHOUGHTS

As I wrote this book, I recognized some common patterns:

- Coincidence and both good and bad luck–being in the right or wrong place at the right or wrong time–play a larger part in our lives than I had previously realized.

- We live on a beautiful planet–why are we destroying it?

- Animals and pets are very important in people's lives. How similar animal behavior and human behavior seems to be.

- Technology has totally changed our lives in the past 50 years. I can't believe how many of my stories would have been different if I'd owned a cell phone. And I can't believe how easy it was to access information for this book on the computer. Those who have spent most of their lives without computers and cell phones appreciate the information age. Those who have grown up with this technology have no idea how different life was without it.

- The speed with which technology has been advancing in the past ten years leads me to say with some trepidation: WOW, what's next? If you are interested in detailed information on the growth and speed of technology, I recommend *Thank You for Being Late–An Optimist's Guide to Thriving in the Age of Acceleration* by Thomas L. Friedman.

- "Things" change–life is not static.

- Life can be funny. "Things" happen that are so bizarre that you can't make them up.

The author loves to share stories. If you have tales to tell and would like to include them in her story repository, please email them to joellenbard@gmail.com. The author retains the right to reject or edit stories. All stories will remain anonymous and there will be no monetary remuneration for participation, but you will be kept informed if your story is used in a future publication or lecture.

Books may be ordered from Amazon.com.

www.ingramcontent.com/pod-product-compliance
Lightning Source LLC
Chambersburg PA
CBHW071903290426
44110CB00013B/1268